Depression

Depression

Henny H. Kim, *Book Editor*

David L. Bender, *Publisher*
Bruno Leone, *Executive Editor*
Bonnie Szumski, *Editorial Director*
Brenda Stalcup, *Managing Editor*
Scott Barbour, *Senior Editor*

Contemporary Issues
Companion

Greenhaven Press, Inc., San Diego, CA

Library of Congress Cataloging-in-Publication Data

Depression / Henny H. Kim, book editor.
     p.   cm. — (Contemporary issues companion)
   Includes bibliographical references and index.
   ISBN 1-56510-889-2 (lib. : alk. paper). —
ISBN 1-56510-888-4 (pbk. : alk. paper)
   1. Depression, Mental. I. Kim, Henny H., 1968–   . II. Series:
Opposing viewpoints series (Unnumbered)
RC537.D426 1999
616.85'27—dc21   98-21728
                                                           CIP

2/2000 Gen fund 18⁰⁰
©1999 by Greenhaven Press, Inc.
P.O. Box 289009, San Diego, CA 92198-9009

Printed in the U.S.A.

Contents

Chapter 4: The Debate over Antidepressants

FOREWORD

In the news, on the streets, and in neighborhoods, individuals are confronted with a variety of social problems. Such problems may affect people directly: A young woman may struggle with depression, suspect a friend of having bulimia, or watch a loved one battle cancer. And even the issues that do not directly affect her private life—such as religious cults, domestic violence, or legalized gambling—still impact the larger society in which she lives. Discovering and analyzing the complexities of issues that encompass communal and societal realms as well as the world of personal experience is a valuable educational goal in the modern world.

Effectively addressing social problems requires familiarity with a constantly changing stream of data. Becoming well informed about today's controversies is an intricate process that often involves reading myriad primary and secondary sources, analyzing political debates, weighing various experts' opinions—even listening to first-hand accounts of those directly affected by the issue. For students and general observers, this can be a daunting task because of the sheer volume of information available in books, periodicals, on the evening news, and on the Internet. Researching the consequences of legalized gambling, for example, might entail sifting through congressional testimony on gambling's societal effects, examining private studies on Indian gaming, perusing numerous websites devoted to Internet betting, and reading essays written by lottery winners as well as interviews with recovering compulsive gamblers. Obtaining valuable information can be time-consuming—since it often requires researchers to pore over numerous documents and commentaries before discovering a source relevant to their particular investigation.

Greenhaven's Contemporary Issues Companion series seeks to assist this process of research by providing readers with useful and pertinent information about today's complex issues. Each volume in this anthology series focuses on a topic of current interest, presenting informative and thought-provoking selections written from a wide variety of viewpoints. The readings selected by the editors include such diverse sources as personal accounts and case studies, pertinent factual and statistical articles, and relevant commentaries and overviews. This diversity of sources and views, found in every Contemporary Issues Companion, offers readers a broad perspective in one convenient volume.

In addition, each title in the Contemporary Issues Companion series is designed especially for young adults. The selections included in every volume are chosen for their accessibility and are expertly edited in consideration of both the reading and comprehension levels of the audience. The structure of the anthologies also enhances accessibility. An introductory essay places each issue in context and provides helpful facts such as historical background or current statistics and legislation that pertain to the topic. The chapters that follow organize the material and focus on specific aspects of the book's topic. Every essay is introduced by a brief summary of its main points and biographical information about the author. These summaries aid in comprehension and can also serve to direct readers to material of immediate interest and need. Finally, a comprehensive index allows readers to efficiently scan and locate content.

The Contemporary Issues Companion series is an ideal launching point for research on a particular topic. Each anthology in the series is composed of readings taken from an extensive gamut of resources, including periodicals, newspapers, books, government documents, the publications of private and public organizations, and Internet websites. In these volumes, readers will find factual support suitable for use in reports, debates, speeches, and research papers. The anthologies also facilitate further research, featuring a book and periodical bibliography and a list of organizations to contact for additional information.

A perfect resource for both students and the general reader, Greenhaven's Contemporary Issues Companion series is sure to be a valued source of current, readable information on social problems that interest young adults. It is the editors' hope that readers will find the Contemporary Issues Companion series useful as a starting point to formulate their own opinions about and answers to the complex issues of the present day.

INTRODUCTION

The term depression is often used to refer to transient feelings of sadness or a case of the "blues." However, depression is more accurately used to describe serious and long-term symptoms, including a persistent sad or empty mood, fatigue, sleep disturbances, eating disruptions, feelings of guilt or worthlessness, and thoughts of death or suicide. Clinical depression's debilitating symptoms and ongoing presence in many people's lives places it well within the class of a mental illness needing a cure. The National Institute of Mental Health (NIMH) estimates that as many as 17 million Americans each year suffer from depression. About one in twenty-five of these sufferers is under the age of eighteen, and one in seven women will experience depression in her lifetime. Depression carries harmful effects that persist for years in those stricken with the disease. The illness strikes regardless of age, gender, class, culture, or ethnic background. Still, many who are depressed do not seek treatment, either because they are unaware that their condition can be helped or because they are all too aware of the stigma and shame associated with depression.

The latter situation is especially true in the workplace. Many professionals who suffer from depression but who appear outwardly high-functioning feel compelled to hide their struggle with the illness for fear that they will lose their jobs or hurt their reputations. As Neasa Martin, executive director of the Mood Disorders Association of Metropolitan Toronto, explains, "People lose credibility. They lose legitimacy when they're identified as having a mental illness, even a treatable mental illness." According to Susan Blumenthal, assistant U.S. surgeon general and deputy assistant secretary for health in the Department of Health and Human Services, "Depression is an illness that is very much misunderstood. It is one of the most pressing public health problems in the country today, yet people still view depression as a character flaw." However, the public understanding of depression has been gradually changing. "There is now general agreement that a variety of factors, both biological and experiential, contribute to depression," according to the *Harvard Women's Health Watch*.

Research concerning the biological causes of depression has made significant inroads in the past few decades, particularly in the area of brain chemicals and their effect on mood. Scientists have discovered that low levels of certain chemicals in the brain, including serotonin, can lead to depression. As knowledge of brain chemistry has increased, new or improved treatments for depression have been introduced, including a new class of antidepressants named selective serotonin reuptake inhibitors (SSRIs). SSRIs such as Prozac, Zoloft, and Paxil regulate the amount of serotonin in the brain, thereby stabilizing the patient's mood and alleviating the effects of depression. In addition, SSRIs have a relatively low rate of adverse side effects compared to previous classes of antidepressants, which has encouraged physician prescriptions and patient endorsements of SSRIs.

In his 1993 best-seller *Listening to Prozac,* psychiatrist Peter Kramer noted the remarkable changes Prozac brought about in depressed patients and pondered the formidable power behind the new class of antidepressants. As his book made its way into public consciousness, so too did ongoing debates concerning antidepressants, the nature of depression, and the most effective way of treating depression. Before the widespread use of SSRIs, common forms of treatment included psychoanalysis (or "talk therapy"), a class of antidepressants called monoamine oxidase (MAO) inhibitors, and electroconvulsive therapy (ECT), more commonly known as shock treatment. Although ECT was used mostly as a last resort on severely depressed patients, the treatment gained a negative reputation as being readily used for any "illness" from excessive creativity to rebellious outspokenness. In addition, ECT's use as a last resort offered no real solutions for those who suffered from milder forms of depression. Psychoanalysis, on the other hand, bore a high price tag and often took years to make any effect on patients' mood. MAO inhibitors, while effective as antidepressants, introduced the possibility of lethal overdose. Compared to these options, SSRIs offered what seemed like miraculous results: few side effects, speedier elevation of mood, and a kind of "emotional band-aid" that helped patients gain more benefits from short-term talk therapy.

Not everyone embraced this new mood drug, however. In fact, almost as soon as Prozac began its climb in popularity, so too did opposition to the drug's prominent role in personality change. In *Talking Back to Prozac,* published a year after Kramer's book, psychiatrist Peter Breggin decried the growing dependence of psychiatry (and subsequently that of patients) on pharmaceutical companies and lamented the erosion of long-term psychotherapeutic approaches to treating depression. In addition, Breggin provided accounts of various patients whose experience with Prozac was as life-transforming as those in Kramer's observations—but rarely for the better. In fact, Breggin charged that Prozac caused extreme violence in some people and ultimately destroyed the lives of these patients and their families. As Breggin warns, although Prozac and other antidepressants have been touted by the media, not every depressed person will react to these drugs in a positive way. Documented cases involving erratic personality changes in Prozac users indicate the need to treat these drugs with utmost caution and careful consideration.

Over a decade after SSRIs were introduced, their use has surged worldwide. While new classes of SSRIs are in the process of being approved for public use, old debates continue and new debates emerge.

The ever-increasing use of antidepressants on children has been discussed in major publications. A movement toward natural healing has gained strength, augmented by the attention given to Saint John's Wort (hypericum), a natural herb reported to relieve symptoms of depression. Meanwhile, many professionals in the field of psychiatry and psychology are urging a balance of therapies, combining what may appear more natural (talk therapy, herbal remedies, exercise and nutrition) with synthetic yet undoubtedly effective treatments.

Depression: Contemporary Issues Companion covers many of these therapies and a wide range of other topics concerning the disease. In the chapters that follow, discussions focus on various types of depression, personal narratives from people who have experienced depression in some form, possible treatments for the illness, and the debate over the use of antidepressants. The selections contained in this volume offer a comprehensive overview of both the scientific and social aspects of depression.

CHAPTER 1

WHAT IS DEPRESSION?

Depression Is a Major Illness

Dianne Hales and Robert E. Hales

In the following selection, excerpted from their book *Caring for the Mind: The Comprehensive Guide to Mental Health*, health writer Dianne Hales and physician Robert Hales provide an overview of depression's causes and symptoms. According to the authors, depression is a frequently unacknowledged and untreated illness that affects millions of people. Major depression, which persists for two weeks or longer, is often accompanied by changes in mood, thought, behavior, and physiological processes, the authors write. They explain that the causes of depression are difficult to pinpoint but are commonly attributed to biological and psychological factors. Because depression afflicts men and women of all ages and every racial and economic group, the authors conclude, a comprehensive understanding of the serious nature of this illness is essential.

Ever since his girlfriend broke up with him, a college student has spent most of the time alone, brooding, not interested in any of the activities he used to enjoy. A young lawyer, convinced that she is not as smart and capable as others think, feels overwhelmed and inadequate. A research scientist snaps at his wife and children and criticizes everything his postdoctoral trainees do. Every winter a librarian finds herself craving rich, creamy foods and becoming so lethargic that she can hardly move. A somber bookkeeper describes herself as "living under a cloud."

Although feelings of depression, sadness, or discouragement occasionally tug at all of us, these individuals are experiencing something quite different: a state of psychological misery that does not go away. Like millions of others with depressive disorders, they have lost their joy in living. Food, friends, sex, and other forms of pleasure may no longer appeal to them. They may be unable to concentrate on their work or fulfill responsibilities. They may fight back tears throughout the day and toss and turn through long, empty nights. Gloom settles over their world like a thick, gray fog, creating an inescapable sense of deep sadness and utter hopelessness.

Unfortunately, fewer than one in every three depressed people ever seeks treatment. One reason is that many Americans still do not think of depression as a real illness that can and should be treated. In a poll by the National Mental Health Association, 43 percent of those surveyed said that they believed depression was a personal or emotional weakness rather than an illness, and blamed themselves, family members, friends, or circumstances for their symptoms. They are wrong.

Comparing everyday "blues" to *clinical depression* (a term commonly used to refer to any depressive disorder that requires treatment) is like comparing a cold to pneumonia. A manager laid off from his job may feel like a failure and not want to see anyone for a few days. A teacher whose mother is dying may have problems fighting back tears in class. Both *feel* depressed, but neither *is* depressed in the sense of having a mental disorder. However, if withdrawal or bouts of overwhelming sadness persist and intensify, clinical depression may develop. . . .

Major Depression

Among the most common problems of the mind, major depression consists of a depressed mood or a loss of interest or pleasure in usual activities that persists for two weeks or longer. In addition, individuals with this disorder typically develop other symptoms, including:

- *Changes in mood:* feeling sad, empty, hopeless, worried, irritable
- *Changes in thinking:* loss of interest or pleasure in usual activities, poor concentration, low self-esteem, indecisiveness, preoccupation with death, thoughts of suicide, guilt
- *Changes in behavior:* slowing down or increased restlessness, crying, social withdrawal, suicidal acts
- *Changes in physical condition:* increased or decreased appetite, disturbed sleep, decreased sexual drive, weight loss or gain, pain, digestive problems, fatigue.

Major depression can develop at any age or stage of life. The incidence of this problem has soared over the last two decades, especially among young adults. Its symptoms can take many forms. Rather than feeling depressed, some people may become pessimistic, irritable, angry, or hostile. One person may chiefly be troubled by a loss of appetite, physical ailments, poor sleep, and lethargy. Another may be plagued by a sense of hopelessness, guilt, and feelings of worthlessness. Others may find that they cannot concentrate or think clearly, that it is hard to be around other people, and that thoughts of death or suicide keep pushing into their minds.

Types of Major Depression

Major depression can be mild, moderate, or severe. Mild cases involve a minimal number of symptoms (five are required for a diagnosis of major depressive disorder) and very little interference with normal functioning at work or in usual social activities and relationships.

Individuals with moderate depression experience more symptoms and greater impairment in their daily lives. In severe depression, symptoms are increased in both number and severity, and take a much greater toll on the ability to function socially or professionally. In extreme cases, individuals are unable to work or even to feed or clothe themselves or to maintain basic hygiene.

Therapists identify three special forms of major depression as melancholic, atypical, and psychotic. Individuals with melancholic depression feel sad in a way they describe as different from other experiences of depression. They typically wake before dawn and cannot return to sleep; their depression is most intense in the morning. Many feel agitated or slowed down. They lose their appetite and weight loss often occurs. Their lack of pleasure in life's normal joys is complete and persistent. When something good happens they don't feel better, even briefly, and they may be haunted by excessive or unfounded guilt.

Individuals with atypical depression, in contrast, are capable of joy, however fleeting, and can feel temporarily happy in response to a pleasurable occurrence. Rather than losing their appetite or being unable to sleep, they may eat and sleep much more than usual. Some report a heavy, leaden feeling in their arms and legs. Often they have a chronic and extreme sensitivity to rejection that interferes with their ability to work and socialize.

In psychotic depression, which is uncommon, individuals lose touch with reality and may develop hallucinations, usually reflecting their sense of doom. They may think their insides are rotting out, for instance, or hear voices telling them to kill themselves. Treatment with antipsychotic medications is often essential.

How Common Is Major Depression?

Young children, teenagers, men and women of every age and every social, racial, ethnic, and economic group can develop depression. According to epidemiological data from the National Institute on Mental Health (NIMH), 4.4 percent of Americans—about 9.4 million in all—develop major depression at some point in life. The National Comorbidity Survey found that major depression is the single most widespread mental disorder, affecting 10.3 percent of Americans in any given year.

At highest risk are those who have already experienced an episode of major depression, who have close relatives with severe depression, or who abuse alcohol or other drugs. Some researchers believe that many who abuse alcohol or drugs do so to ease or mask depression.

Women are two to three times more likely than men to develop major depression, dysthymia (chronic mild depression), seasonal affective disorder, or recurrent brief depression. According to the *Diagnostic and Statistical Manual of Mental Disorders, Fourth Edition (DSM-IV)*, a woman's lifetime risk for major depression ranges from 10 to 25 percent in community samples, compared with 5 to 12 percent for men. Rates for men and women are highest between the ages of twenty-five and forty-four years, The average age at onset is the mid-twenties.

In recent decades, major depression has been increasing and developing earlier in life. Epidemiological reports from China, Canada, France, Lebanon, New Zealand, and other countries indicate that the incidence of depression among individuals younger than age twenty-five is rising worldwide. Researchers have theorized that urbanization, a breakdown in family ties and traditional religion, and a rise in drug and alcohol abuse may be contributing factors.

An estimated 15 percent of adults over the age of sixty-five—and up to 25 percent of nursing home residents—have symptoms of major depression. In the elderly, physicians and family members often attribute many symptoms of depression to medical causes. A National Institutes of Health (NIH) panel of experts has warned that more than 60 percent of older Americans suffering from depression are not receiving appropriate therapy, often because both health care providers and individuals themselves misinterpret sad feelings as a normal response to the medical, social, and economic problems the elderly face. In other circumstances, what appears to be depression in the elderly may have physical roots, such as poor nutrition or anemia.

Depressed individuals may wonder, "Why did this happen?" or "Why do I feel this way?" Unfortunately, there are no definitive answers. Like many other illnesses, major depression can strike out of the blue without apparent reason. Various combinations of different factors—biological, genetic, chemical, psychological, social, developmental, and environmental—may lead to major depression. As with so many medical conditions, some individuals appear to have a biological vulnerability that makes them especially susceptible. Nevertheless, whatever its origins, depression is an illness characterized by neurochemical abnormalities that cause significant disability. It can be deadly, and it must be recognized and treated.

Biological Factors

Extensive research into the neurobiology of depression has shown that depression is a complex biological illness that affects the delicate balance of brain chemicals, the signaling system used for communication between neurons, the flow of blood through the brain, the hormones that regulate dozens of body processes, and the mechanisms involved in sleep and wakefulness.

• *Heredity* The parents, siblings, and children of persons who have suffered major depression are more likely than others to become depressed themselves. In general, the rate of depression among close relatives is 1.5 to three times that of individuals with no family history of depression.

Studies of identical twins, who share identical genes, have suggested a genetic basis for depression. If one identical twin becomes depressed, the other faces a much greater chance of depression. In a study of more than a thousand pairs of female twins, the risk for an identical twin developing depression if her sister had the disease was 66 percent higher than the risk in the general population. Among fraternal twins, the risk was 27 percent higher. Children whose biological parents were depressed, and who were adopted at birth into families with no history of the disorder, are more likely to develop depression than the biological children of their adoptive parents. However, heredity is not the only determinant. Individuals with no family history also can and do develop major depression.

• *Brain chemistry* Depression alters the balance of certain crucial chemicals within the brain, including neurotransmitters, or messenger chemicals, such as serotonin and norepinephrine, that allow brain cells to communicate with each other.

In the past, scientists theorized that deficiency in either serotonin or norepinephrine or both may lead to depression. This hypothesis now seems simplistic. Other neurotransmitters may also be involved, or the underlying problem may stem from alterations in certain types of receptors, the specialized molecules that receive messages sent from neuron to neuron. In addition, some scientists studying depression are investigating the role of other brain chemicals, including the neuropeptides (short-chain amino acids that perform some of the same functions as the traditional neurotransmitters).

• *Hormonal systems* In addition to disrupting brain chemistry, depression may interfere with virtually every function of the endocrine system. It can cause subtle abnormalities in the production of hormones by the hypothalamus and the pituitary and adrenal glands. Many depressed persons have abnormal thyroid function. Sometimes psychiatrists give supplements of the thyroid hormone T_3 (not T_4, which is a treatment for hypothyroidism) to individuals who do not improve with antidepressants alone.

• *Sleep-wake controls* Depression has been linked with disruptions in the sleep-wake mechanisms within the brain. Depressed individuals often show characteristic changes in their sleep patterns, particularly a tendency to enter rapid eye movement (REM) or dream sleep much earlier in a night's sleep than usual. Researchers have been experimenting with sleep deprivation as a possible way of enhancing response to antidepressant drugs, speeding up their impact, preventing recurrences of the disorder, or predicting whether an individual will improve with treatment with a specific drug or electroconvulsive therapy (ECT).

Psychological Factors

Depression is an illness of the mind as well as the brain, and many theories about its psychological origins have emerged over the years.

Freud traced adult depression back to childhood loss, a theory he later discounted. Many of his successors elaborated on this idea, arguing that loss, if not fully acknowledged and mourned, can result in sadness, anger, hopelessness, extreme sensitivity to rejection, and low self-esteem. Individuals who cannot express anger or assert their independence, often for fear of rejection or abandonment, may punish themselves for such "unacceptable" feelings by turning the anger inward and becoming depressed.

Therapists disagree as to whether some individuals have characteristic ways of behaving that put them at greater risk of depression. However, it has been observed that those who seek help for depression often share certain characteristics: Many are unable to fend off negative thoughts, have unrealistic expectations and standards for their own performance, or depend excessively on others. Having made a series of "safe" but unrewarding life choices, such people may end up in circumstances that provide little joy or satisfaction—with a dead-end job, an unloved mate, and overwhelming family responsibilities.

• *Cognitive and behavioral factors* According to the creators of cognitive therapy, depression stems from a negative way of thinking about self, the environment, and the future. Automatically assuming that they, their world, or their future lacks something essential for happiness, individuals come to view themselves as inadequate or unworthy, their families as critical or unsupportive, and their prospects as bleak. Negative, distorted thoughts become more frequent as depression deepens.

Individuals who feel inadequate or unworthy may be particularly vulnerable to the sort of distorted thinking that can lead to depression. Their attitudes and reasoning processes lead them to faulty conclusions about the world and their own self-worth. They may also lack the social skills necessary to obtain positive feedback, such as praise for a job well done. Even when someone does compliment them, they may not believe they deserve the kind words.

Based on experiments with animals, psychologist Martin Seligman, Ph.D., developed the behavioral theory that past experiences of real helplessness (such as suffering from an accident or injury) can convince individuals that they will not be able to control current or future difficulties. As a result of such "learned helplessness" they become passive and resigned, accepting painful situations as inevitable and feeling overwhelmed and helpless.

• *Stress and life traumas* Numerous or intensely stressful life events have often been linked with the development of depressive disorders, although they seem to have an impact primarily on initial episodes of major depression. Severe or unanticipated stress, major losses (such as the death of a loved one, a divorce, or the loss of a job), family or marital problems, financial problems, a move to a new town, a life transition (such as having a child), and chronic illness may trigger a first attack. But even among individuals facing similar amounts of stress, some seem inherently more vulnerable to depression than others.

Grief following the greatest possible life trauma—the death of a loved one—may lead to symptoms of depression, and if it becomes particularly intense or prolonged it can develop into major depression. A bereaved person who has not begun to move on with life within six months, who becomes preoccupied with feelings of guilt or worthlessness, who develops hallucinations or delusions, or who contemplates suicide may have slipped into a major depression and needs treatment.

A lack of stable, close relationships may increase susceptibility to depression. Spouses (especially women) who describe their marriages as being in trouble are much more likely to be depressed than those in happy ones. Problems involving relationships may contribute to a woman's vulnerability. Men, who make up a third of depressed individuals, tend to get depressed for different reasons. Socialized to place great importance on being good providers and achievers, they are more likely to become depressed after the loss of a job, a promotion, or professional status. Paradoxically, success can have the same effect as failure for those who feel they don't deserve it or can't meet expectations. Some high achievers become depressed because they miss the challenge and stimulation of fighting their way to the top. For both men and women, ongoing tension or pressure, particularly in jobs that provide few rewards and little security, can set the stage for depression.

How Major Depression Feels

Developing a major depression is like falling into a bottomless pit. Although sufferers want to escape, they cannot muster the strength to move. They want to understand how they got there, yet they cannot concentrate or think clearly. Cut off by their depression from all they once cherished, they find that they simply don't care anymore. They feel themselves sliding into deeper, more terrifying depths, but they cannot help themselves or even hope that someone else might help them. They see no way out, and they may spend hours or days brooding about their past failures or future trials. . . .

Consumed by their own misery, depressed individuals pull away from others, isolating themselves within walls of apathy, indifferent to those around them. A loving mother no longer cuddles her children. An avid tennis player no longer picks up a racquet. Even a long-awaited event, such as an exotic vacation, sparks no excitement. Life's pleasures are beyond reach, too remote to touch or even tempt. Very often individuals lose all interest in sex and pull away from any form of intimacy.

The face in the mirror turns into a despicable character with countless faults and no redeeming virtues. A straight-A student feels incapable of keeping up with schoolwork. A devoted spouse reproaches himself for every short-tempered remark. A hardworking manager accumulates evidence of her own incompetence. Guilt over current or past failings grows steadily. The most trivial incident, such as a forgotten errand, becomes further proof of inadequacy. When anything goes wrong, depressed individuals blame themselves. Even when they are clearly not responsible, they are guilty in their own eyes.

Often men react differently to depression than women. Denying the problem, men try to keep going and shake it off because they view it as a weakness. Far more than women, they mask their depression with irritability, since anger is an easier emotion than sadness for many men to express. They frequently self-medicate by drinking, but the depressant nature of alcohol only pulls them further down.

Yet both sexes suffer—and suffer deeply. "I am now the most miserable man living," Abraham Lincoln wrote during one of his depressions. "If what I feel were equally distributed to the whole human family, there would not be one cheerful face on earth." Baffled by what is happening within them, depressed individuals may wonder if they are losing their minds. Their families may share the same terrible fear.

Depression Alters Behavior

Major depression distorts internal timing. A person may speak less or more slowly, pause longer before answering, speak in soft or monotonous tones, even stop talking at all. Some individuals move more slowly while others become incapable of sitting still. One woman recalls pacing back and forth day after day in her tiny apartment, wringing her hands as she walked.

Sleep patterns are shattered. Often a depressed person will sleep fitfully for a few hours and then wake long before dawn, unable to get more rest. Others will have the opposite response and sleep far more than usual, sometimes logging twelve or more unrefreshing hours in bed. Because depression saps vitality and stamina, getting out of bed in the morning seems a great burden. Routine tasks such as making dinner are exhausting. Any extra demand, such as getting an appliance or car repaired, may seem overwhelming.

The altered brain chemistry of depression can slow and cloud thought processes. Individuals often find it difficult to focus, remember, concentrate, make decisions, or think through an issue. They may be easily distracted. Some people find it hard to absorb information or carry on a casual conversation. They read a newspaper without assimilating a single sentence or forget a question they have just been asked. Nothing lightens the load they feel.

Typically, depressed people lose their appetite and interest in food. Many shed ten pounds or more without any attempt at dieting. Conversely, some individuals, particularly women, crave sweets or other carbohydrates and eat more when they are depressed, often in binges. Those who put on a good deal of weight feel even worse about themselves.

Depressed individuals often have other psychological symptoms, including obsessive brooding, excessive concern about physical health, panic attacks, or phobias. Anxiety may be a symptom of depression or may develop at the same time. This combination, which creates profound suffering at the core of one's being, can be lethal, since high levels of anxiety in depressed individuals may increase the risk for suicide.

But the pain of depression is never simply psychological. "Mysteriously, in ways difficult to accept by those who have never suffered it, depression comes to resemble physical anguish," William Styron writes. "Such anguish can become every bit as excruciating as the pain of a fractured limb, migraine, or heart attack."

As major depression deepens, thoughts of death may push ever more insistently into consciousness. Individuals may become preoccupied with death and wish they could succumb to a fatal illness or die in an accident. Some, assuming that their loved ones would be better off without them, contemplate what had once seemed unthinkable—ending their own lives.

Seeking Help

Many depressed individuals do not realize that they are seriously ill. Some blame themselves and try to "tough it out"; others turn to alcohol or drugs. The inertia and despair bred by major depression keep many from obtaining help. Without treatment, they may suffer for months or even years. Often family members must take the initiative in seeking help because the depressed person may be too emotionally "stuck" to do so—or to recognize the need for it. Loved ones must reach through the isolation, show their concern, and encourage a depressed individual to go for help.

Major depression can develop over days or weeks or can occur suddenly, usually after a trauma. Some people experience mild symptoms or feelings of anxiety for several months before plunging into depression. Others experience relatively brief periods of depression that recur at least once a month.

The primary reason to suspect depression is a change from previous feeling and functioning that persists for most of the day, nearly every day, for two weeks or more. The most common symptom is feeling discouraged, sad, or hopeless—and not feeling better with some rest or relaxation, the passage of time, or good news. Major depression always affects the way a person works, copes with everyday tasks, and relates to others.

If you or someone close to you has not been able to function normally for two weeks or more, these are the questions that should be asked:
- Do you feel sad, anxious, tearful, irritable, or hopeless for most of the day, almost every day?
- Have you lost interest in eating, sex, socializing, or your favorite activities?

- Are you eating more or less than usual? Have you gained or lost weight?
- Are you sleeping more or less than usual?
- Do you feel as if you're talking or walking in slow motion? Do you fidget constantly or find yourself incapable of staying still?
- Are you always tired? Are you too weary to tackle even small chores?
- Do you feel worthless or guilty about something?
- Are you having problems in thinking, concentrating, or making decisions?
- Have you been thinking more and more about death? Do you ever think you'd be better off dead? Have you thought about killing yourself?

Many people will answer "yes" to at least one of these questions. If you are feeling down, you might respond "yes" to two or three, perhaps four. If you answer "yes" to more than four questions, you may need professional help. Keep in mind that depression is one of the most curable diseases of mind or body—but the key to getting better is getting help.

A Broader, Better Understanding of Depression

Joe Chidley

Until recently, Joe Chidley writes, many people considered depression a character flaw, and therefore the disease carried a considerable amount of social stigma. However, with the use of antidepressants becoming widespread and an abundance of public figures speaking out about their own afflictions, the general public's view of depression is changing, he explains. A significant increase in the amount of readily available information and important developments in the treatment of the illness have made it easier for sufferers to learn about and cope with their condition, Chidley concludes. Chidley, who writes frequently about psychology and neuroscience, is a staff writer for *Maclean's*, a weekly Canadian news magazine.

The first serious bout was back in 1963, when he was attending Queen's University and, just before final exams, locked himself in his dorm room for two weeks. The next came seven years later, when he was Vancouver bureau chief for *The Globe and Mail:* he dismantled the bell on his office and home telephones ("So no one could reach me, but I could still dial out," he recalls), and spent his days playing tennis and walking under the Burrard Street Bridge, contemplating suicide. The last time it happened, in September 1993, it made the veteran journalist and seeming bon vivant the talk of Toronto media circles: what happened to Joey Slinger? After 14 years of writing a four-times-weekly humor column in *The Toronto Star*, Canada's largest-circulation newspaper, Slinger suddenly disappeared. Rumors abounded about how he quit in a huff, about him working as a clerk in a downtown bookstore—both true, it turns out. But what few of Slinger's readers and acquaintances suspected was that, behind his evaporation from the *Star*'s pages lay a disease with which he has struggled for much of his life. "Every now and then, I have what used to be called a nervous breakdown," says Slinger, 54. "Now, it's called depression."

That, thankfully, is not as shocking an admission as it once was. In the nearly 10 years since the release of Prozac—the first and most pub-

Reprinted from Joe Chidley, "Depression: Society Comes to Grips with a Devastating Disorder," *Macleans*, December 1, 1997, by permission of the publisher.

licized of the so-called SSRI (for selective serotonin reuptake inhibitor) family of drugs—there has been a revolution in the treatment of depression, and in the way many people think about it. Even well into the 1970s, depression was primarily considered a character flaw or a result of poor upbringing, to be treated with Freudian on-the-couch psychoanalysis. Now, researchers are approaching a deeper under- standing of how depression affects the brain, and of its potential physical and genetic underpinnings. At the same time, a revolution of a different sort has begun among sufferers, fuelled in part by public admissions of celebrities—among them, U.S. media mogul Ted Turner, *60 Minutes* co-host Mike Wallace, Canadian actress Margot Kidder and singer-poet Leonard Cohen—that they, too, have mood disorders. There is a new openness about the condition, and an increasing recog- nition of its economic costs, as employers and insurance companies grapple with a boom in disability claims and absenteeism due to depression. And today more than ever, sufferers can find support in their communities, as hundreds of self-help groups have sprung up across Canada, allowing them to talk about their illnesses and the challenges they face in an open, sympathetic atmosphere.

A Widespread Illness

Finally, depression is coming out of the closet. But it still has a long way to go. The statistics on depression make the old saw about misery loving company seem like a cruel joke. More than 24 million people worldwide now take Prozac, just one of the five SSRIs. By conservative estimates, more than one million Canadians every year will suffer from any one of about a dozen depressive disorders, ranging from dysthymia (low-grade, chronic depression) to so-called bipolar affec- tive disorder or manic depression, which causes radical mood swings between emotional highs and the depths of despair. In fact, many doctors who treat depression think there is more of it around, although some say it just seems so because the illness is being recog- nized and treated more often than in the past. Still, theories abound about why depression might be spreading. Some experts blame high levels of stress in industrialized societies, or suspect that environmen- tal chemicals may be to blame. "People cite the divorce rate, the decline in religion, the role of television," says Dr. Jane Garland, director of the mood disorders clinic at the British Columbia Chil- dren's Hospital in Vancouver. "Take your pick."

The tragedy of depression is compounded by the fact that it remains widely misunderstood. True, everyone gets the blues. And the classic symptoms are well-known: loneliness, feelings of inadequacy, worthlessness, anxiety, a longing for death. But anyone who has been spared the experience of what Winston Churchill—another famous depressive—called his "black dog" cannot fully grasp the anguish depression brings. It is simply "hell on wheels, emotionally terrorizing," says one manic-depressive, who asked not to be identified. "That's why people kill themselves, and unless you've experienced it, you *cannot* imagine."

Slinger's last bout of severe depression began several weeks before his "disappearance." Professionally, he recalls, he had hit "a really bad spell of the dries, like bone grinding against bone. I would find myself sitting at the word processor crying, and I thought, 'This is terrible, I'm gonna electrocute myself.'" In September 1993, he went on a canoeing trip in the Northern Ontario wilderness of Temagami—and decided to pack in his career, calling his boss from a pay phone. Luckily, then-managing editor Lou Clancy and editor John Honderich gave Slinger a year's leave-of-absence rather than accepting his resignation. In that time, he wrote a book on bird-watching, worked part time at a bookstore, and started taking Luvox, one of the SSRI drugs. "It was wonderful," he says. "To me, it's a miracle drug."

Slinger returned to writing his column in 1994, and now says he takes Luvox only when he feels a depressive episode coming on. "The key to me is that I start thinking about suicide," he explains. "It becomes, all of a sudden and bizarrely, among the things I might do today—'I might get a haircut, I might go to a movie, I might kill myself.'" But after 30 years of on-again, off-again depression—and with an effective treatment in hand—Slinger says he has learned to accept his disorder, and to live with it. "I'm satisfied this is something that just happens to people, like diabetes."

A Balancing Act

Thousands of others, however, are not so fortunate. Many with depressive disorders struggle for years—and often for their whole lives—to find the right balance of drug therapy, counselling and community support to help make their illnesses manageable. That runs counter to the popular notion about Prozac and other antidepressants which, given all the media attention paid them over the past decade, might be mistaken as a *cure* for depression. "The new medications have made a spectacular difference," says William Ashdown, a depressive himself and president of the Winnipeg-based Mood Disorders Association of Canada, a public-education and self-help organization. "But there's no rhyme or reason to these diseases, and that's a tremendous challenge for some people. They're looking for a cookie-cutter illness, and there's just no such thing."

In the vast majority of cases, treatment of depression *does* work: doctors concur that up to 90 per cent of people with depressive disorders will respond to therapy. The irony is that depression is so rarely treated: experts estimate that only one-third of sufferers receive appropriate therapy. Misdiagnosis or lack of treatment is particularly acute among the elderly. According to researchers, only a quarter of people over 65 who have severe depression are adequately treated.

The reasons are complex. Physical ailments can mask symptoms of depression—often confused, in turn, with Alzheimer's disease—and that can make it difficult to diagnose. But there are social factors, too, and an incipient belief, even in the medical community, that depression is simply a fact of life for the elderly. Another problem, says Dr. Cesar Garcia, a geriatric psychiatrist at York County Hospital in Newmarket, Ont., is that many elderly patients are uncomfortable talking about emotional problems. "There's a real stigma for that age group about psychiatry and about depression," he says.

Depression comes in many forms, but the one thing that sufferers young and old confront is the stigma, the fear or outright antipathy still directed at the mentally ill. It prevents many from seeking help in the first place. And it can make sufferers—even those receiving proper treatment—lead a double life. Wendy, a community outreach worker in western Canada in her mid-50s, has lived with bipolar disorder for much of her adulthood. Her first bout of severe depression occurred at 19, when she stopped eating and lost 35 lb., stopped sleeping and had repeated thoughts of suicide. At the time, her doctor suspected she was pregnant. "And I said to him, 'Pregnant? I haven't even *looked* at a boy.'" Times have changed. And now, Wendy—who has been responding well to treatment for the past 13 years—is "living a good life." In her job, she gives support to other people with depressive disorders. She is frank about her illness—but not with everyone. In fact, like most sufferers, she prefers that her real name not be published; she does not even want her home town identified. And she still keeps two résumés on file, one (which she used to get her current job) that describes her condition, and one that does not. "I've accepted my illness, and encourage others to do that, too," says Wendy. "But not everyone accepts this—it could be held against me some day."

The Cost Is High

As a social problem, depression is devastating in its economic and personal consequences. The national mood disorders association estimates that direct and indirect medical costs of depression in Canada top $5 billion a year, and depression in the workplace is proving an enormous burden to insurers and to businesses: absenteeism due to the illness costs Canadian companies an estimated $2.3 billion annually in retraining, restaffing and lost productivity. But that's only money. The more telling figure: about 3,500 Canadians take their own lives every year—and another 50,000, by conservative estimates—attempt to. Although the forces behind suicide are varied, depression is believed to be responsible for between 60 and 90 per cent of those deaths.

When Doris Sommer-Rotenberg, a 71-year-old writer, poet and jewelry designer, talks about her son Arthur, she knows she sounds like a doting mother. "But he was a remarkable young man," she explains. "He was a doctor, a wonderful athlete—he had everything. But he also had this dreadful illness." The illness was bipolar disorder, or manic-depression, diagnosed at the age of 17. When he was well, his mother recalls, he "was great fun, and had such a love of life." But in 1992, Arthur suffered a deep depression. Doris Sommer-Rotenberg says she did not understand the significance of a visit he paid to her that fall at her downtown Toronto home. "In retrospect," she says, "I think he came to say goodbye."

In November 1992, 36-year-old Arthur took his own life. But his mother was not content to let her son become a statistic. In January 1997, the University of Toronto—matching the $1 million she helped to raise through private and corporate donations—established the Arthur Sommer-Rotenberg Chair in Suicide Studies, the first of its kind in North America, and chose psychiatrist Dr. Paul Links, an authority on suicide's causes and prevention, as the first incumbent. For Sommer-Rotenberg, the chair is a way of keeping her son's spirit alive. And although suicide among people with bipolar disorder is startlingly common, with a rate of about 25 per cent, she believes that deaths like her son's could be prevented with more understanding and research. "Some doctors might say no," she says. "But I think any suicide is preventable. I have to."

Needing Support

Among people with depression, it is a common refrain—the sense of being alone. "Friends and family try to be supportive, but at a certain point it is hard for them to help or know what to say," says Sara, a 33-year-old freelance writer in Montreal who suffers from dysthymia. "When someone compliments me, it doesn't sink in—they might as well be talking about the weather." Often, too, advice given with the best intentions can do more harm than good. "Some people say, 'Why don't you get out of bed, snap out of it? You've got a good job and a lovely home—just get on with it,'" says Wendy in western Canada. "But if we *could* do that, wouldn't we?"

Just two decades ago, there were few places for people with depressive disorders to turn for support—besides family, friends or psychotherapists. But that is changing. In early 1983, five men and women in Winnipeg—including Ashdown's ex-wife—got together to discuss their illnesses at the prompting of their psychiatrist, Dr. Jim Brown. So began the Society for Depression and Manic-Depression of Manitoba, the oldest self-help group for mood-disorders sufferers in the country. From it sprang a host of other groups, in a wave that can only be described as a self-help revolution. Today, there is a national association, regional organizations in every province except New Brunswick, Prince Edward Island and Newfoundland (plans are under way to start them there, too), and as many as 800 other support groups scattered across the country, from small towns to major cities.

Collectively, the self-help groups provide information to people with depressive disorders and their families. Ashdown says the Manitoba office fields about 5,000 telephone calls, holds 150 high-school information sessions, and has some 500 self-help meetings every year. Part of the organizations' function, he adds, is to educate the public about depression, and do what they can to counter the lingering stigma. But their central role is to provide support to people who are confused, frightened or ashamed by their illnesses. "An individual goes to a doctor, gets treated, usually gets little or no explanation of what it means to him, and is then left alone to face the fact that he is now designated as a mental patient," says Ashdown, 46. "Self-help organizations fill a huge gap."

Dealing with Life

To the volunteers who work for self-help groups, they can also provide a sense of purpose. Eva, from Thornhill, is 50. But she has struggled with her disease since she was 17, when she was an A student, pretty, with plenty of boyfriends—and suddenly "began to feel so, so sad." At 19, she became seriously depressed, and was hospitalized for six weeks. Diagnosed with bipolar disorder 10 years later, she has experienced it all: the medication (she has taken lithium for 21 years, now combined with another mood stabilizer, Tegratol), the cost to her personal life (her first marriage ended in divorce after five years, when she was 23), and the pervasive misconceptions of people around her, even her parents. "I'm still told by my parents that I'm not depressed, I'm lazy," Eva says. "That hurts."

Despite all the obstacles, however, Eva is coping. A big part of that, she says, is her work with the Mood Disorders Association of Metro Toronto where for 10 years she has volunteered as a facilitator for twice-monthly self-help meetings, attended by sufferers and their families. The diseases vary, from dysthymia and major recurring depression to bipolar disorder, but common themes arise: problems with work, medications, doctors and spouses. "It's not people talking down to you, or who have just read something in a book," says Eva. "It's people who have been there." Educating other sufferers' families, she stresses, is important. "I felt there was not much I could do in my own situation, so I tried to do it for others," she says. "It feels good when people say, 'Thank you.'"

In many ways, Eva's is a good-news story. In person, she is warm and funny, with a sparkling intelligence. She has had a successful career and raised two children, who she says are very supportive and informed about her illness. And she has achieved a delicate balance of drugs, psychotherapy and self-help: for the seven years since her last bout of depression, her mood has been stable. In that time, she divorced her second husband, sold her house and moved into a condominium, and underwent major surgery on her hip. Now, she is planning to begin a new career as an events planner, and she has started dating again—a nerve-racking experience for any 50-year-old. But Eva is nothing if not determined. "I've had times in my life when I've felt like a little child," she says. "But I don't want to depend on anybody, on my children or on my parents. I want to depend on myself." Given the anguish she has endured, that is a courageous stand. And proof that, while the war against depression is far from over, those who struggle with the disease can still achieve something significant: a life worth living.

Shedding Light on Seasonal Affective Disorder

Norman E. Rosenthal

Norman Rosenthal is the director of light therapy studies at the National Institute of Mental Health and the author of *Seasons of the Mind* and *Winter Blues: Seasonal Affective Disorder: What It Is and How to Overcome It*, from which the following selection is excerpted. The seasons generally carry emotional associations, Rosenthal writes; for example, spring is considered to be rejuvenating while winter is seen as cheerless. However, he notes, some people find that seasonal changes produce significant alterations in their moods. Rosenthal discusses the scientific experiments that led to the discovery that certain individuals only experience depression during months with less daylight, a condition known as seasonal affective disorder (SAD). He also describes the use of light therapy to treat SAD.

Like the bears, squirrels, and birds, humans have evolved under the sun. We have incorporated into the machinery of our bodies the rhythms of night and day, of darkness and light, of cold and warmth, of scarcity and plenty. Over hundreds of thousands of years, the architecture of our bodies has been shaped by the seasons, and we have developed mechanisms to deal with the regular changes that they bring. We continue to respond to these rhythms in the way we feel and behave. For some of us, however, these changes can disrupt our lives.

The effects of the seasons on humans were all well known by the ancients, but were largely forgotten by modern medical practitioners until recently. Their importance was kept alive through the centuries by artists, poets, and songwriters. Shakespeare, for example, observed that "a sad tale's best for winter," while Keats wrote of a nightingale singing of summer "in full-throated ease," and the singer of a modem ballad calls his beloved the sunshine of his life.

In the past fifteen years, science has caught up with the arts, and the medical importance of the seasons has been recognized anew. Surveys have shown that most people experience some alteration in mood or behavior with the changing seasons, and that for as many as one in four persons, these changes are a problem. Natural and effective treatments have been developed to help people with marked seasonal problems, known as Seasonal Affective Disorder, or SAD. We are also aware of a milder version of this condition—the "winter blues"—and other forms of the condition, such as summer depression. Over the same period, our understanding of the emotional impact of the seasons—of light and temperature—has advanced. We are now better able to understand our relationship to the physical world around us. . . .

There are indeed seasons of the mind, though they are not the same for everyone. Autumn may enchant some with its grand colors, but for others it carries the threat of winter. Winter, cheerless and forbidding for many, has associations with stagnation, decay, and loss. But some people experience a different type of winter—one that finds them snug and cozy by the fireside, with chestnuts popping. Spring brings buds and blossoms, rebirth, with sap stirring, feverish urges, and a longing to go on pilgrimages. But we are also told that "April is the cruelest month . . . mixing memory and desire." Summer yields a harvest of fruit and flowers, but in the words of the Bard, "sometimes too hot the eye of heaven shines." Had they heeded the words of the poets, twentieth-century physicians would have realized much sooner that the seasons can have a profound effect on the way we feel, and that we react to changing seasons in different ways.

States of mind evoked by the seasons and the weather form part of our language. A person is said to have a "sunny disposition," a "radiant smile," to be "warm" or "cold." Every news program carries a section on the weather. Our curiosity about the weather goes far beyond wanting to know whether to take along an umbrella or not. The weather and the changing seasons affect the way many of us feel, how we sleep, what we eat, whether we can concentrate on our work, and even whether we are able to love.

This idea seems so obvious now that it is hard to believe that there was a time when we paid no heed to the effects of the changing seasons on humans. Only twenty years ago, when I was in medical school, we were taught nothing about the effects of the seasons. According to the view handed down to us, human beings were seasonless creatures. Electricity provided us with light and heat. Food was available all year round. We were not like other animals, which have to cope with the challenge of the changing seasons.

Had we studied the ancients, we might have recognized that a seasonless view of human physiology and behavior is incorrect. Hippocrates, for example, observed in the fourth century B.C. that "whoever wishes to pursue the science of medicine in a direct manner must first investigate the seasons of the year and what occurs in them." Many physicians who followed him emphasized the effects of the different seasons on the mind and body. Apparently that wisdom was buried by the wonders of the Industrial Revolution. We forgot that we were once much closer to nature than we are today. We didn't realize that achieving some mastery over our physical environment did not eliminate our responses to the changing seasons, which are presumably programmed into our genetic code.

Artificial methods of escape from darkness, cold, moisture, and extreme heat have provided us with considerable protection from the effects of the seasons on our bodies, minds, and spirits. With this protection, the changing seasons are for many people merely the backdrops against which to go about their daily business. But others experience them with extreme intensity. Perhaps among these people are poets and artists who have seen the changing seasons as metaphors for our lives—whose emotional surges have produced some of the most beautiful products of the human mind.

However, there are also those for whom seasonal transitions trigger extreme changes in mood and energy, and produce sadness and despair. . . .

My Own SAD Story

I trained as a doctor in South Africa—a country that, for all the turbulence of its politics, can truthfully boast about its climate. In Johannesburg, where I grew up, there were really only two seasons: summer and winter. During summer you could swim outdoors and eat summer fruit: peaches, papayas, mangoes. During winter you could not do these things. It was warm outdoors during the day, though at night you needed a sweater. Spring and autumn were transition times. After several months of winter the blossoms would appear, and you knew it was spring. Similarly, when the long summer was over, the leaves would turn a simple brown and fall off the trees without much fuss or fanfare, and winter was there. But despite the mildness of the seasons, I was aware at some level of the effect they had on my mood. I had even considered writing a novel in which the mood of the central character changed regularly with the seasons. The novel was never written, but the seed of the idea stayed with me, germinating quietly. It required the intense seasonal changes of the higher latitudes to which I moved to activate that kernel of thought; it also required my encounters with some inspiring people, who are central to this story. I arrived in the United States in the summer of 1976 and began both my psychiatric residency at the New York State Psychiatric Institute and research into disorders of mood regulation. The summer days felt endlessly long, and my energy was boundless. I had never experienced such long summer days in Johannesburg, which is much nearer to the equator than New York City.

As the months passed, I was struck by the drama of the changing seasons. I had been unprepared for the brilliant colors of the autumn leaves in the north, the crisp days and cold nights, and—most of all—for the disappearance of the light. I had not anticipated how short the days would be. When the sun shone, its rays struck the earth at a strange, oblique angle, and I understood what the poet Shelley meant when he wrote:

Bright Reason will mock thee
Like the sun from a wintry sky.

Then daylight saving time was over and the clocks were put back an hour. I left work that first Monday after the time change, and found the world in darkness. A cold wind blowing off the Hudson River filled me with foreboding. Winter came. My energy level declined, and I wondered how I could have undertaken so many tasks the previous summer. Had I been crazy? Now there seemed to be no alternative but to hang in and try to keep everything afloat. I understood for the first time the stoic temperaments of the northern nations. Finally, spring arrived. My energy level surged again, and I wondered why I had worried so over my work load.

I registered all these impressions, but I did not put them together into a cohesive story—and I probably would never have done so, had it not been for the events that followed and the remarkable people I was to meet. At the end of my residency I went to the National Institute of Mental Health (NIMH) in Bethesda, Maryland, to undertake a research fellowship with Dr. Frederick Goodwin, whom I had heard speak on the topic of manic-depressive illness from both biological and psychological points of view. Dr. Goodwin made the subject come alive, describing how our shifting moods and fluctuating perceptions of the world correspond to certain changes in our brain chemistry. Since mind and brain seemed equally fascinating frames of reference, I wanted to use both models to try to understand mood disorders.

Shortly before my first visit to the NIMH, I met Dr. Alfred Lewy, one of several psychiatrists working with Goodwin at the time. Dr. Lewy had just developed a technique to measure the hormone melatonin, in collaboration with Dr. Sanford Markey. Melatonin is produced by the pineal gland, a pea-sized structure tucked underneath the brain. Each night, like clockwork, the pineal releases melatonin into the bloodstream in minute quantities, and continues to do so until dawn. The secretion of melatonin signals the duration of darkness, and thus serves as an important seasonal time cue in animals. Although it is unclear whether melatonin is instrumental in causing seasonal changes in humans, the research in this area proved to be a critical step in the rediscovery of SAD and light therapy.

Dr. Lewy and I spoke about our common interests and the various directions in which our research might take us. On occasion we chatted over a mass spectrometer, the instrument he had used to develop his technique for measuring melatonin. It looked like a very large washing machine. He injected samples of clear fluid into a small hole in the top, and reams of paper rolled off it, while inked pens traced out a graph upon the paper. He pointed to one blip on the graph and said, "That's melatonin." I was suitably impressed.

After I joined Goodwin's group, I was assigned to work most closely with Dr. Thomas Wehr, an outstanding clinical researcher, who had for some years been studying biological rhythms in an attempt to learn whether abnormalities in these rhythms might be at the basis of the mood disturbances in depression and mania. Shortly before my arrival at the NIMH, Drs. Lewy and Wehr had shown that bright light was capable of suppressing the secretion of human melatonin at night—a finding that was to have great influence over the events that followed. There was a buzz in Goodwin's group at chat time—a sense of excitement—and I felt certain I had come to the right place.

A Light-Sensitive Scientist

Although many people were responsible for the rediscovery of SAD, our steps toward this end can all be traced back to the actions of one man: Herb Kern. In some ways, Herb might have appeared to be an unlikely person to initiate a new area of medical investigation, for he was not himself a medical professional, but a research engineer with a major corporation. I met Herb a year after I arrived at the NIMH. At sixty-three, he was a youthful-looking man with a wiry build, a crew cut, and a twinkle in his eyes. He was intensely curious, and he had noted in himself a regular pattern of mood and behavioral changes going back at least fifteen years. A scientist by nature and training, he had kept careful notes of these changes in numerous small notebooks. He observed that each year, from July onward, his energy level would decline and he would withdraw from the world. At these times he lacked energy, had difficulty making decisions, lost interest in sex, and felt slowed down and "ready for hibernation." He found it difficult to get to work in the morning, and once there he would sit at his desk, fearful that the telephone would ring, obliging him to have a conversation with someone. It is typical for a depressed person to withdraw—to have neither the desire nor the energy to interact with others. In fact, in many cases, he or she may feel that it is an impossible task. People who are depressed simply want to be left alone.

More bothersome to Herb than his social isolation was the decrease in his creative powers during his depressed periods. He would procrastinate at work because "everything seemed like a mountain" to him, and his productivity decreased markedly. It was only by grim perseverance that he was able to write up his studies from the previous spring and summer. His sleep was disrupted, and his characteristic enthusiasm for life evaporated.

The months would drag on like this for Herb until mid-January, when, over a two-week period, his energy would return. As he put it, "The wheels of my mind began to spin again." He had ample, even excessive energy at these times, and needed little sleep. Ideas came freely, and he was eager to communicate them to others. For five or six months he was very confident of his abilities and felt that he could "tackle anything." He was very efficient and creative, needed only four hours of sleep per night, was more interested in food and sex, and admitted to a "tendency to go overboard" in buying luxuries.

Herb had observed that his mood improved as the days lengthened and declined as they shortened, and he had actually developed a theory that this might be due to changes in environmental light. He attempted to interest several people in his hunch that his mood and energy levels were related to the time of year. One of these, Dr. Peter Mueller, a New Jersey psychiatrist in private practice who had a research background, listened to Herb and subsequently looked for other patients with a similar history. Herb was treated with several different antidepressant medications, all of which resulted in unacceptable side effects without correcting his symptoms. Herb eventually read about the work of Drs. Goodwin, Wehr, and Lewy and found his way to the NIMH, where he asked us to work with him on his seasonal difficulties.

Dr. Lewy suggested that we treat Herb by lengthening his winter day with six hours of bright light—three before dawn and three after dusk—in an attempt to simulate a summer day. He reasoned that since bright light is necessary for melatonin suppression in humans, it might similarly be necessary for altering mood and behavior. This reasoning was based on two pieces of information. First, the secretion of melatonin is an important chemical signal for regulating many different seasonal rhythms in animals. Second, the nerve pathways involved in the suppression of melatonin secretion by light pass through parts of the brain that we believe are important in regulating many of the physical functions that are disturbed in depression, such as eating, sleeping, weight control, and sex drive. If the suppression of melatonin required much brighter light than ordinary indoor fixtures provided, then perhaps bright light might also be necessary in order for the brain to perform other mood-related functions.

We asked Herb to sit in front of a metal light box, about two feet by four feet. The box emitted as much light as one would receive while standing at a window on a spring day in the northeastern United States. We chose full-spectrum fluorescent lights—a type that mimics the color range of natural sunlight coming from a summer sky—in order to replicate the conditions that appeared to bring Herb out of his winter depressions. . . .

Within three days, Herb began to feel better. The change was dramatic and unmistakable. He was moving into his spring mode several weeks ahead of schedule. Did we dare to hope that we might have found a new type of treatment for depression? Intriguing as this possibility was, our excitement was immediately tempered by our scientific instincts. After all, Herb had had a heavy emotional investment in the light therapy. Might his response not have been due to something other than the light—the wish to feel better, for example, or the emotional impact of entering an experiment in which three research psychiatrists were studying the outcome of a treatment based on his ideas? This possibility—the so-called "placebo effect"—had to be seriously considered. The placebo effect has dogged behavioral researchers for years, and we could not rule it out in evaluating the antidepressant effects of light therapy on Herb.

A Human Bear

During the same winter that Herb was receiving light treatment at the NIMH, Dr. Mueller, in consultation with Dr. Lewy, tried artificial light treatment with another patient, whom I will call "Bridget." She also appeared to benefit from light, and had an unusually good winter that year. The following summer, as luck would have it, Bridget moved to the Washington metropolitan area, and Mueller suggested that she contact us. Bridget's history and ingenuity in fitting the details of her seasonal problems into a coherent story were as remarkable as Herb's. She described herself as a "human bear."

She was a professional in her mid-thirties, who had been aware of disliking winter since childhood. But it was not until her early twenties that a regular pattern of seasonal changes emerged. Bridget's problem would begin each year in August or September, as she anticipated the forthcoming winter with increasing anxiety. She was mystified about what subtle cues might be causing her premonitory dread, since this feeling began during the summer, when the days were still warm. She wondered whether it might be the fall catalogs, with their pictures of winter clothes, that triggered the memories of unpleasant winters of earlier years. Regardless, when the leaves began to change color, she would have a strong urge to take out her winter clothes and stock her cupboards with food, "like a squirrel getting ready for winter."

As winter approached, Bridget experienced many symptoms similar to those described by Herb, such as feelings of extreme fatigue, a leaden sensation that made her want to lie down and sleep all day long. She would overeat at these times, and observed a marked craving for sweets and starches. As in Herb's case, Bridget continued to struggle in to work each day, though her productivity declined markedly. In addition to her seasonal mood problem, Bridget also felt depressed and irritable for a few days before each menstrual period, regardless of the season. When spring arrived, her depression lifted and was replaced by elation. In her earlier years she would forget her winter difficulties once they were over. "I was like the grasshopper," she remarked (referring to the fable about the grasshopper and the ant), "singing and playing all summer long," indifferent to the next winter that was to come.

Bridget had also observed that other changes in the environment besides the seasons seemed to affect her mood. She had visited the Virgin Islands during the two winters before her first light treatment. Both times she had been impressed by the marked improvement in her mood just days after her arrival on the islands, and the relapse a few days after her return to the north. She had lived for some years in locations at different latitudes: Georgia, New York, and Quebec. The farther north she lived, the earlier her depression began, the more depressed she felt, and the later her remission in the spring was. She began to suspect that something in the environment was influencing her mood, and that perhaps it was the light. Why else did she seem to crave it so? Why else did she hate her poorly lit office? She made up any excuse to seek out the brightly lit photocopying room. Light treatment made good sense to Bridget. She was eager to try it and was delighted to find that it worked for her.

In Search of SAD

Unusual individual cases have historically played an important role in medical research in general, and psychiatry in particular. We wondered whether Herb and Bridget might be examples of a special seasonal kind of depression, and whether they might help us understand how others respond to the changing seasons and environmental light.

Although single cases may be of great importance in generating new hypotheses, we generally need groups of patients to test them experimentally. Dr. Mueller said that he had encountered several other patients with seasonal depression. We wondered how common the problem was. Were there any other such patients in the Washington, D.C. area who might be interested in participating in a research program? I called a few local psychiatrists who specialized in treating depression, but they said they had not encountered the problem. I concluded that it must be quite rare and that the only chance we had of finding such a group was by publicizing our interest in the *Washington Post*.

Sandy Rovner, a journalist who specializes in health issues, sat across the room from me, tape recorder in hand, and listened to my story. She decided that it would be of interest to her readers and wrote an article for the *Post*, which launched an entire field of research. Rovner's article began with Bridget's own words: "I should have been a bear. Bears are allowed to hibernate; humans are not."

The response to the article took us all by surprise. Instead of hearing from a handful of afflicted people, we received thousands of responses from all over the country, and our phones rang for days. We sent out screening questionnaires, which were returned by the hundreds. I read them with a growing sense of excitement. In psychiatric research, "heterogeneity" is a major problem; in other words, the same condition may differ greatly in character from one patient to another. This has proven to be an enormous obstacle to psychiatric researchers, especially in the area of schizophrenia. As I read the questionnaires, it seemed as though Bridget had been cloned, as one person after another reported the symptoms of the condition that we went on to call SAD. I wondered whether this similarity in symptoms might correspond to a similar underlying disturbance in brain chemistry, which might imply a favorable response to light, as we had observed with Herb and Bridget.

We interviewed many people and admitted into our program all those with clear-cut histories of winter depression. During that summer, as expected, all the participants felt well and showed an unusually high level of energy. This generated considerable skepticism among some of my colleagues, who speculated that we might be dealing with a group of suggestible people who had read the article and persuaded themselves that they had the syndrome. That seemed unlikely to me, but I had no way of disproving it. I could not help feeling sightly uneasy when one of my colleagues pointed out that if none of the participants became depressed when winter arrived, we would all look a little foolish.

The First Controlled Study of Light Therapy for SAD

The days grew shorter, and in October and November, right on schedule, the participants began to slow down and experience their winter syndromes, just as they had described. Although I was clearly not affected to the same degree as my seasonal patients, I noticed that I too had to push myself harder to get anything done. It was more difficult to get up in the morning, and even the project did not seem so exciting as it had the previous summer.

We planned to treat the patients with light as soon as they became moderately depressed—just enough so that we would be able to measure an effect of the treatment, but not to such a degree that they felt incapacitated. We decided to use full-spectrum light, as we had with Herb Kern, for three hours before dawn and three hours after dusk. In any experiment designed to show the effectiveness of a treatment, it is important to have a "control" condition—one that incorporates all the ingredients of the "active treatment" condition, except the one believed to be crucial for achieving the desired effect. In this study we believed that the brightness of the light would be crucial, so we used dim light as a control. In order to make the control treatment more plausible, we chose a golden-yellow light—a color associated with the sun, and one to which the eye is highly sensitive.

We treated each patient with two weeks of bright light and two weeks of dim light, then compared the effects. This type of treatment design—called a "crossover" because the individual is "crossed over" from one treatment condition to the other—has since been used widely for light therapy studies. We presented the two conditions to the patients in random order. In other words, some began with the bright white light and others with the dim yellow light, so as not to bias the outcome. It is also important for psychiatrists evaluating the effects of a treatment not to be aware of which treatment a patient has received, so that their prejudices cannot be reflected in their ratings. For this reason, the treatment conditions were known only to me, not to my collaborators in this study, Drs. Wehr, David Sack, and J. Christian Gillin.

I will never forget the first patient who underwent the bright light treatment—a middle-aged woman, markedly disabled by SAD. During the winter she was barely able to do her household chores, get to work, or attend her evening classes. After one week of treatment, she came into our clinic beaming. She was feeling wonderful and keeping up with all her obligations. She also mentioned that her classmates were regarding her with a new competitive respect as she answered questions in her evening classes, as if to say, "Where have you been hiding all this time?"

The second patient who received the bright light condition was treated around Christmas. I called the ward from New York City, where I was spending the holiday with friends, and asked Dr. Sack how things were going with the study. He replied, "I don't know what treatment 'Joan' is receiving, but she's blooming like a rose."

And so it went. Nine patients responded to bright light, and the dim light proved ineffective. I began to use the lights myself and was sure that they made me feel better. Some of my colleagues requested them, too. After a few weeks I had to put a big sign in front of the dwindling stack of light boxes, asking anyone who wanted to borrow a fixture to discuss it with me first so that we would have enough for the study. A local psychiatrist, whom I had initially polled about the existence of SAD patients (and who had told me that he did not know of any), called to say that he had realized that he himself had the syndrome, and asked about how he might use the lights himself.

Many questions were raised by the results of our first study. Was it really possible that light was affecting mood? Could there be some explanation for the improvement, other than the light itself? Was it all a placebo effect? And if it was the light, how was it working? These were all important questions, and in due course, we and other researchers would address them, one by one. But as we reviewed the study in the spring of 1982, we realized that the patients had become depressed during fall and winter, as they had predicted they would. The light treatment had worked more dramatically than we had ever hoped it might. The azaleas and the dogwoods were in bloom. Spring had arrived and, at that moment, nothing else seemed to matter very much either to our patients or ourselves.

In the years that followed, we continued to treat new waves of SAD patients each winter, as did researchers at other centers. Light studies performed in other parts of the United States, Europe, and Japan corroborated our experience. SAD is common, and light treatment works. In view of this general consensus, the American Psychiatric Association recognized a version of SAD in its diagnostic manual, *DSM-III-R* [the *Diagnostic and Statistical Manual of Mental Disorders*], in the spring of 1987. In a brief six years since the first SAD patients were treated with light, a variant of depression that appeared at first to be a rare curiosity was recognized by the psychiatric community as an important clinical condition.

DYSTHYMIA: THE PERSISTENT BLUES

Maura Rhodes

According to Maura Rhodes, people who constantly feel down and dreary often attribute these moods to their personality. However, Rhodes points out, this condition actually may be a chronic mild depression called dysthymia. She writes that dysthymia is frequently undetected because of its subtle and long-ranging symptoms, affects more women than men, and persists for two years or longer. While dysthymia does not debilitate a sufferer in the way severe depression might, its deleterious effects still takes its toll on sufferers' self-esteem and general outlook, asserts Rhodes. Fortunately, she notes, help is available, most frequently in the form of antidepressants or psychotherapy. Rhodes is a staff writer for *McCall's*, a monthly women's magazine.

Rose Wagner is living the kind of life sitcoms are made of: At 41, the New York City resident has a devoted husband, a pampered pooch named Bosco and a quirky, satisfying job photographing people with their pets. This is quite a change from 1982 when, soon after moving to Manhattan from Wisconsin, Wagner developed a relentless case of the blues. A clothing-store manager at the time, Wagner had never considered herself especially moody—she enjoyed socializing and going out and had plenty of energy. "But in New York, I was under a lot of stress, and I began to notice I couldn't handle the day-to-day grind. It was hard to focus and concentrate, and I was drained by the end of the day," she recalls. "On weekends I preferred sleeping to taking a walk. It reached the point where I wasn't even up to going to the movies with my boyfriend."

Wagner's tenacious dreary mood lingered—for 12 long years. Despite it, she married, switched careers and adopted Bosco, all the while believing her glumness to be "just the way I was." It wasn't until 1994, while she was watching a television program about depression, that she realized she might need a medical boost to help her out of the doldrums. After seeing a psychiatrist, Wagner was diagnosed with a form of chronic mild depression called dysthymia (dis-THIGH-mee-uh), also known as dysthymic disorder.

Reprinted, with permission, from Maura Rhodes, "When You Can't Beat the Blues," *McCall's*, October 1996.

A Subtle Disorder

Dysthymia, which means, literally, "ill-humored," affects up to 5 percent of the population of the United States, according to the National Institute of Mental Health. Most people diagnosed with dysthymia are between the ages of 15 and 54, and the malady is twice as common in women as it is in men, although this may be because women are more likely to report their symptoms, says Kay Redfield Jamison, Ph.D., a professor of psychiatry at the Johns Hopkins University School of Medicine in Baltimore. Jamison is the author of *An Unquiet Mind*, a book about her own battle with manic depression.

Yet, pervasive as dysthymia is, many who struggle with it spend years being misdiagnosed and mistreated simply because they mistake their symptoms for personal shortcomings or personality quirks. "Dysthymia causes you to think there's something wrong with your character," explains John C. Markowitz, M.D., an associate professor of clinical psychiatry at Cornell University Medical College in New York City. "You're likely to think, 'I'm just a bad person.'"

When the Zest for Life Fades

It wasn't until 1980 that psychiatrists began offering medical treatment for this disorder. That was the year dysthymia was classified as a form of depression, thanks to a major overhaul of the *Diagnostic and Statistical Manual of Mental Disorders*, or *DSM* (the criteria developed by the American Psychiatric Association to define mental illnesses). According to the *DSM*, dysthymia is a depressed mood that occurs for most of the day, on more days than not, and persists for two years or longer. In addition, at least two of these symptoms are present:
* Poor appetite or overeating;
* Insomnia or sleeping too much;
* Fatigue or low energy;
* Low self-esteem;
* Poor concentration;
* Difficulty in making decisions;
* Feelings of hopelessness.

While dysthymia is rarely incapacitating, "it puts a glass ceiling on life," says Michael E. Thase, M.D., a professor of psychiatry at the University of Pittsburgh School of Medicine. "You're unable to enjoy yourself, have fun or experience pleasure. You may feel shy or embarrassed around others, and you procrastinate because you're afraid of failing or because you have no energy."

"You might not achieve your full potential at work, believing you're not being promoted because you don't deserve it," adds Kimberly A. Yonkers, M.D., an assistant professor in the department of psychiatry and of obstetrics and gynecology at the University of Texas Southwestern Medical Center at Dallas. "You may not get married, or you may not feel satisfied with your marriage."

When the Blues Will Not Go Away

Given this broad and somewhat vague spectrum of symptoms, it's easy to see how dysthymia can go undetected. Often it takes a crisis to alert sufferers to the fact that they have a problem: Because they lack the self-esteem, energy or optimism needed to pull through hard times, as many as half of those who have dysthymia are driven to episodes of severe sadness when faced with significant adversity. This compounds the illness, resulting in a situation called double depression.

Sandy Marincic, 33, of North Huntingdon, Pa., experienced this vulnerability when, within two years, she lost her live-in boyfriend, relocated because she had landed a new job, then lost the position. (Name and some details have been changed for privacy.) Rotten as her luck had been, "the worst part was I had to find another job, make decisions. I was paralyzed," she recalls. While most people would have brooded for a few weeks, then started picking up the pieces, Marincic sank into a deep funk. Severely depressed, she finally answered an ad for a research study of antidepressants at the University of Pittsburgh and learned she was dysthymic.

"I realized I had suffered from the blues all my life," she says. "Thinking back, I could remember only two periods during childhood when I actually felt good. I was lethargic and unhappy at my job. I accepted all this as my lot in life."

Dysthymia can have a variety of causes. For some sufferers, early adversity—say, growing up with an alcoholic parent—sets them up for depression. For others, a chronic disease, such as arthritis, may send them into a tailspin. But for many, the predisposition to depression may be biological. "There's likely to be a family history of depression," says Thase.

Good News: Help Is on the Way

Fortunately, medication is effective for relieving the problem. It worked for Claudia Myers, 33, of San Carlos, Calif. With a loving marriage, two wonderful kids and a challenging, satisfying career as an attorney, Myers is a shining example of the fact that a woman can have it all. Yet even as a child, Myers was moody. "I didn't act the way most kids did. Things bothered me," she recalls. "I always felt angry and frustrated, and I cried a lot in private. I remember when I was eight, a cousin I hardly ever saw got married, and I developed an overwhelming sense that she was abandoning me. I cried for weeks after the wedding."

As an adult, Myers continued to be down on herself, down on life and angry to boot. "I thought I was just being crabby," she says. Despite her misery, though, she succeeded in some areas: "I had no social life, but I did pass the CPA exam, and I went to law school."

It wasn't until after she was married and had had her first baby that Myers recognized something might be seriously wrong. Following the baby's birth, her glumness metamorphosed into sob-inducing depression, and her anger turned almost violent. Then Myers read an article listing the symptoms of depression and realized that what she had always thought was just the blues might in fact be a treatable illness. After being diagnosed with dysthymia at a psychiatric clinic, she then participated in a drug trial for the antidepressant imipramine and soon began feeling better. "It was as if someone were literally taking a weight off my shoulders," says Myers, who is now on Prozac (fluoxetine). . . .

While antidepressants rarely become permanent residents in the medicine chest, people must continue taking them for a period of time after they feel better, to prevent a relapse. Many antidepressant users experience long-term improvement after having taken the drug for four to six months; others need more than one course of treatment.

Talk Therapy

In addition to medication, psychotherapy—talk sessions with a trained professional—can also banish the blues. But of the over 250 kinds of psychotherapy currently practiced, only two seem to work for dysthymia, according to Markowitz. Both deal with the here and now rather than delving into a patient's childhood. *Interpersonal therapy* aims at improving your mood by helping you learn to cope with events that are fueling your current depression, such as the loss of a loved one. *Cognitive therapy* teaches you to recognize and correct negative thinking. Your therapist may ask you to write down self-defeating thoughts you have, so you can review the list together.

"Cognitive therapy simply boils down to reevaluating your conception of who you are and how you see the world," says Sandy Marincic of her experience. "You're asked to prove why you don't feel you're worth as much as other people. When, after about 20 minutes, you've finished talking yourself in circles, you realize your perception is skewed. Then you apply that realization to living."

As researchers continue to find out which drugs and forms of psychotherapy are most successful, treatment for dysthymia may become even more effective. But the mere fact that the condition now has a name is providing great relief to countless women who otherwise would have chalked up their misery to nonexistent shortcomings. Instead, many feel as satisfied as Rose Wagner, who is "happy, motivated and at peace."

CHAPTER 2

DIMENSIONS OF DEPRESSION: PERSONAL NARRATIVES

YOUNG AND DEPRESSED

Elizabeth Wurtzel

In her book *Prozac Nation: Young and Depressed in America*, Elizabeth Wurtzel describes her lifelong battle with depression, including a disturbing history of suicide attempts and self-mutilations. In the following excerpt from her book, Wurtzel writes about a time shortly after college graduation when her increasingly serious mood swings were regulated by a wide array of antidepressants and other medications, and she depicts the chaos that resulted when she stopped taking one of her drugs. She states that despite her continued attempts to combat her illness, she experienced nervous breakdowns and alienation from her friends and family. Although Wurtzel finally resumed taking her medication, she explains that she was reluctant to do so because of the potentially serious side effects of taking so many drugs.

I start to get the feeling that something is really wrong. Like all the drugs put together—the lithium, the Prozac, the desipramine, and Desyrel that I take to sleep at night—can no longer combat whatever it is that was wrong with me in the first place. I feel like a defective model, like I came off the assembly line flat-out fucked and my parents should have taken me back for repairs before the warranty ran out. But that was so long ago.

I start to think there really is no cure for depression, that happiness is an ongoing battle, and I wonder if it isn't one I'll have to fight for as long as I live. I wonder if it's worth it.

I start to feel like I can't maintain the facade any longer, that I may just start to show through. And I wish I knew what was wrong.

Maybe something about how stupid my whole life is. I don't know.

My dreams are polluted with paralysis. I regularly have night visions where my legs, though attached to my body, don't move much. I try to walk somewhere—to the grocery store or the pharmacy, nowhere special, routine errands—and I just can't do it. Can't climb stairs, can't walk on level ground. I am exhausted in the dream and I become more exhausted in my sleep, if that's possible. I wake up tired, amazed that I can even get out of bed. And often I can't. I usually sleep ten hours a night, but often it's many more. I am trapped in my body as I have never been before. I am perpetually zonked.

Staying in Bed for Too Long

One night, I even dream that I am in bed, stuck, congealed to the sheets, as if I were an insect that was squashed onto the bottom of someone's shoe. I simply can't get out of bed. I am having a nervous breakdown and I can't move. My mother stands at the side of the bed and insists that I could get up if I really wanted to, and it seems there's no way to make her understand that I literally can't move.

I dream that I am in terrible trouble, completely paralyzed, and no one believes me.

In my waking life, I am almost this tired. People say, Maybe it's Epstein-Barr. But I know it's the lithium, the miracle salt that has stabilized my moods but is draining my body.

And I want out of this life on drugs.

I am petrified in my dream and I am petrified in reality because it is as if my dream is reality and I am having a nervous breakdown and I have nowhere to turn. Nowhere. My mother, I sense, has just kind of given up on me, decided that she isn't sure how she raised this, well, this thing, this rock-and-roll girl who has violated her body with a tattoo and a nose ring, and though she loves me very much, she no longer wants to be the one I run to. My father has never been the one I run to. We last spoke a couple of years ago. I don't even know where he is. And then there are my friends, and they have their own lives. While they like to talk everything through, to analyze and hypothesize, what I really need, what I'm really looking for, is not something I can articulate. It's nonverbal: I need love. I need the thing that happens when your brain shuts off and your heart turns on.

And I know it's around me somewhere, but I just can't feel it.

What I do feel is the scariness of being an adult, being alone in this big huge loft with so many CDs and plastic bags and magazines and pairs of dirty socks and dirty plates on the floor that I can't even see the floor. I'm sure that I have nowhere to run, that I can't even walk anywhere without tripping and falling way down, and I know I want out of this mess. I want out. No one will ever love me, I will live and die alone, I will go nowhere fast, I will be nothing at all. Nothing will work out. The promise that on the other side of depression lies a beautiful life, one worth surviving suicide for, will have turned out wrong. It will all be a big dupe.

Everything Went Wrong

It is Saturday night, we're about at that point when it starts to be Sunday morning, and I am curled up in fetal position on my bathroom floor. The black chiffon of my dress against the stark white tiles must make me look like a dirty puddle. I can't stop crying. The twenty or so people who are still sitting in the living room don't seem at all fazed by what's going on with me in here, if they notice at all, between sips of red wine and hits on a joint someone rolled earlier and chugs on Becks or Rolling Rock. We decided—my housemate, Jason, and I—to have a party tonight, but I don't think we meant for two hundred people to turn up. Or maybe we did. I don't know. Maybe we're still the nerds we were in high school who get enough of a kick out of the possibility of being popular that we actually did bring this on ourselves.

I don't know.

Everything seems to have gone wrong. First, Jason opened the fire escape door even though it was the middle of January because it had gotten so hot with the crush of bodies, and my cat decided to make the six-flight climb down into the courtyard, where he got lost and confused and started howling like crazy. I didn't have any shoes on and I was worried for him, so I ran down barefoot and it was freezing and it really shook me up to come back in to so many people I had to say, *Hello, how are you?* to, people who didn't know I have a cat that I am absolutely crazy about. For a while Zap and I hid in my room. He curled up on my pillow and gave me a look like all this was my fault. Then my friend Jethro, seeing that I was scared of all these people, offered to do a run up to 168th Street and get some cocaine, which would maybe put me in a better mood.

Being on so many psychoactive drugs, I don't really mess with recreational controlled substances. But when Jethro offered to get me something that might possibly alter my state just enough so I wouldn't want to hide under the covers, I thought, Sure, why not?

Lithium Withdrawal

There's more: Part of the reason I am so meek is that I stopped taking my lithium a few weeks before. It's not that I have a death wish, and it's not that I'm like Axl Rose and think that lithium makes me less manly (he supposedly stopped taking it after his first wife told him that his dick wasn't as hard as it used to be and that sex with him was lousy; not having that kind of equipment, I'm in no position to give a shit). But I had my blood levels taken at the laboratory about a month ago, and I had an unusually high concentration of thyroid stimulating hormone (TSH)—about ten times the normal amount—which means that the lithium is wreaking havoc on my glands, which means that I could end up in a really bad physical state. Graves' disease, which is a hyperthyroid condition, runs in my family, and the treatment for it makes you fat, gives you these bulging, ghoulish eyes and creates all kinds of symptoms that I think would make me more depressed than I am without lithium. So I stopped taking it. The psychopharmacologist (I like to call his office the Fifth Avenue Crack House, because all he really does is write prescriptions and hand out pills) told me I shouldn't. He told me that, if anything, the lithium was going to give me a condition the opposite of Graves' disease ["What does that mean?" I asked. "Will my eyes shrink up like crinkly little raisins?"), but I don't trust him. He's the pusherman, and it's in his interest to see that I stay loaded.

But he was right. Off lithium, I was fading fast. Some days, I'd sit with Jason reading the *Times* in the living room and I'd talk a blue streak, presenting him with all my theories about, say, the deterioration of the American family in the late twentieth century and how it all relates to the decline of an agrarian society. And Jason would mostly sit there, absorbed in the paper, wondering if I would ever shut up. But then most days I'd be bummed out, plain and simple, ineffectual, going blank again.

Substitute Drugs

I really needed my lithium. But I was determined to cold-kick it. If cocaine would help, so be it. Coke may be really bad for you in every possible way, but it wouldn't give me a thyroid disease, thereby turning me into a younger version of my hysterical, exhausted, overwrought mother. So I did a few lines in the bathroom with Jethro, cutting them up on a Pogues CD. Not five minutes after the stuff first started floating around in my brain, I felt a whole lot better. I went out and mixed and mingled. I walked up to strangers and asked if they were having fun. When new guests arrived, I greeted them, kissing them on each cheek, European-style. I offered to fetch a beer or mix a screwdriver, give them a tour of the apartment, or show them where they should throw their coats. I said things like: There's someone you simply *must* meet. Or, grabbing some girl's hand and pulling her across the room: Have I got the guy for *you*. I was magnanimous and gregarious and all that stuff.

And then, a couple of hours later, I started coming down. I don't drink, so I didn't have any alcohol in my system to take the edge off what was happening. But suddenly, everything turned ugly, grotesque. Spooky holograms all over the walls, like acid flashbacks without the color or wonder or other redeeming features. I felt a panic, as if there were things I needed to do while I was still on a coke high, and I had better do them before I completely dropped off. There was the guy I spent a misbegotten night with who said he'd call me and never did but came to the party anyway, and I felt primed for a confrontation. There was my dad, who I really wanted to call just then, if only to remind him that he still owed me my allowance from the four years in high school when I couldn't find him. There were a zillion other things to do, but I couldn't remember what they were. I knew only that I wanted a few more minutes to live in this charmed, enchanted, wired state. I wanted just a little more time to feel free and easy and unhampered before returning to my depression. I wanted more coke. MORE! COKE! NOW! I started looking around the bathroom to see if there were any little bits of the powder left so I could keep it going.

As I patted my hands around the sink and frisked the floor, I got the weird sense that this sort of behavior maybe had its place in the eighties, but it seemed really stupid right now, completely passé in the ascetic, adult nineties. And then I reminded myself that life is not a media-generated trend, I'll be damned if I'm going to deny myself just because of Len Bias and Richard Pryor and whoever else.

Saturday Night Breakdown

So I'm getting ready to ask Jethro to go back up to Spanish Harlem to get us some more of this stuff. I'm making plans, I'm thinking grandiose thoughts, I'm listing all the people I'm going to call once I'm coked up again and have the nerve. I'm deciding to spend the whole night writing an epic Marxist-feminist study of Biblical villainesses which I've been meaning to get started on for years. Or maybe I'll just find a twenty-four-hour bookstore and get a copy of *Gray's Anatomy* and memorize it in the next few hours, apply to medical school, and become a doctor and solve all my problems and everyone else's too. I've got it all worked out: *Everything is going to be just fine.*

But before any of this can happen, I crumple onto my bed and start to weep uncontrollably.

Christine, my best friend, comes in to ask what's wrong. Other people come in to get their coats, strewn on my bed, and I start snapping at them, telling them to get the hell out. I start yelling at Christine that I want my room back, I want my life back. As if on cue, Zap proceeds to vomit on a coat that apparently belongs to someone named Roland, which seems like just desserts for coming to my party and being part of my awful night.

I have this palpable, absolute sense that I'm cracking up, that there's really no good reason why, and that—even worse—there's nothing I can do about it. And the thing that's really bugging me, as I lie curled up, is that the scene I'm enacting reminds me of something: It reminds me of my whole life.

A Recurring Nightmare

Just outside the French doors leading into my room, Christine and Jason and a few other friends—Larissa, Julian, Ron—are conferring. I can hear them, the whispers of discussion, but they don't sound nearly as concerned and conspiratorial as they might have a few years ago. They've seen me this way before, many times. They know I go through this, I survive, I go on, it could be severe premenstrual syndrome, it could be—in this case it probably is—cocaine blues. It could be nothing.

I can imagine Jason saying: Elizabeth's having one of her episodes. I can imagine Christine saying: She's losing it again. I can imagine them all thinking that this is all about a chemical deficiency, that if I'd just take my lithium like a good girl, this wouldn't happen.

By the time I stumble into the bathroom and slam both doors and curl up tight to the floor, I'm certain that there's no way they'll ever understand the philosophical underpinnings of the state I'm in. I know that when I'm on lithium, I'm just fine, that I can cope with the ebb and tide of life, I can handle the setbacks with aplomb, I can be a good sport. But when I'm off the drugs, when my head is clean and clear of this clutter of reason and rationality, what I'm mostly thinking is: Why? Why take it like a man? Why be mature? Why accept adversity? Why surrender with grace the follies of youth? Why put up with the bullshit?

I don't mean to sound like a spoiled brat. I know that into every sunny life a little rain must fall and all that, but in my case the crisis-level hysteria is an all-too-recurring theme. The voices in my head, which I used to think were just passing through, seem to have taken up residence. And I've been on these goddamn pills for years. At first, the idea was to get me going so I could respond to talk therapy, but now it seems clear that my condition is chronic, that I'm going to be on drugs forever if I just want to be barely functional. Prozac alone isn't even enough. I've been off lithium less than a month and I'm already perfectly batty. And I'm starting to wonder if I might not be one of those people like Anne Sexton or Sylvia Plath who are just better off dead, who may live in that bare, minimal sort of way for a certain number of years, may even marry, have kids, create an artistic legacy of sorts, may even be beautiful and enchanting at moments, as both of them supposedly were. But in the end, none of the good was any match for the aching, enduring, suicidal pain. Perhaps I, too, will die young and sad, a corpse with her head in the oven. Scrunched up and crying here on a Saturday night, I can see no other way.

I mean, I don't know if there are any statistics on this, but how long is a person who is on psychotropic drugs supposed to live? How long before your brain, not to mention the rest of you, will begin to mush and deteriorate? I don't think chronically psychotic people tend to make it to the nursing-home-in-Florida phase of life. Or do they? And which is worse: to live that long in this condition or to die young and stay pretty?

The Tears Keep Falling

I stand up to take out my contact lenses, which are falling out anyway, dripping down a sliding pond of tears. The pair I have on tonight is green, a spare set I got during a buy-one-get-one-free sale, which I wear when I feel like hiding behind a creepy, phony set of eyes. They give me an inanimate appearance like I'm spooked or from another planet or a lifeless Stepford Wife who cooks, cleans, and fucks with a blissful, idiotic smile. Because the lenses are already slipping off of my pupils, it appears that I have two sets of eyes, some sick twist on double vision, and as they slide out I look like a living doll, a horror movie robot whose eyes have fallen out of their sockets.

And then I'm back on the floor.

Jason comes in after everyone has left and urges me to go to bed, says something about how it will all feel better in the morning. And I say, Goddamnit, you asshole! I don't want it to feel better in the morning! I want to deal with the problem and make it better or I want to die right now.

He sits down next to me, but I know he'd rather be with Emily, his girlfriend, or anywhere else. I know he'd rather be washing dishes in the other room or sweeping the floor or gathering cans and bottles for the recycling bin. I know that I'm so awful right now that cleaning is more appealing than sitting with me.

Jason, how long have we known each other? I ask him. What's it been, at least five years, since junior year?

He nods.

And how many times have you seen me like this? How many times have you found me bawling on the floor somewhere? How many times have you found me digging a grapefruit knife into my wrist, screaming that I want to die?

He doesn't answer. He doesn't want to say: Too often.

Jase, it's like twenty-five years already, my whole life. Every so often there's a reprieve, like when Nathan and I first fell in love, or when I first started writing for *The New Yorker*. But then the dullness of everyday kicks in, and I get crazy.

He says something about how when I'm on lithium I seem to be fine. Like that makes it all okay.

I start crying hard, taking little panicked breaths, and when I can talk it's only to say, I don't want to live this life. ‹

I keep crying and Jason just leaves me there.

Julian, who apparently is spending the night because he lost his keys, comes in next. I might as well be Elizabeth Taylor in *Cleopatra*, receiving supplicants on the bathroom floor.

Julian says stuff like, Happiness is a choice, you've got to work toward it. He says it like it's an insight or something.

He says, You've got to believe.

He says, Come on! Cheer up! Pull yourself together!

I can't believe how trite all this is. For a moment I want to step out of myself so I can teach him some better interpersonal skills, so I can help him learn to sound a little more sensitive, more empathic than all this.

But I can't stop crying.

Finally, he picks me up, mumbling something about how all this is nothing a good night's sleep won't cure, saying something about how we're going to go get some lithium in the morning, not understanding that I don't want to feel better in the morning, how that way of life is wearing me out, that what I really want is not to feel this way in the first place. I keep pushing away from him, demanding that he put me down. I am literally doing what people mean when they say, She went kicking and screaming. Poor Julian. I start poking at his eyes to get him to put me down because that's what I learned to do in a course on self-defense for women. Jason hears me screaming and comes in, and the two of them just kind of force me into bed, and I think that if I don't comply, maybe the men in white coats will come with a straitjacket and take me away, a thought that is momentarily comforting, and ultimately, like everything else, horrifying. . . .

Meeting with Dr. Ira

Monday morning, two days after the party, I am back at the Fifth Avenue Crack House, a.k.a. Dr. Ira's office. It's actually about three in the afternoon, but that's early for me.

Dr. Ira is berating me for going off lithium without discussing it with him first. I explain that I panicked, the Graves' disease and all. He explains that the blood tests I get every couple of months monitor me so closely that we would know if there were a problem long before it got out of hand, that we could take necessary steps in advance of such an emergency. He's making sense. I can't and don't argue. Besides, he tells me that the results on a second set of blood levels came out perfectly normal. He thinks the mistake was all about a mis-placed decimal point, a computer error that turned 1.4 into 14. Right now, the TSH level is a perfectly average 1.38.

Of course, I don't know what any of these numbers mean, don't really want to ask. But I can't pull myself away from a nagging suspi-cion that it just can't be this simple. What I mean is this: Prozac has rather minimal side effects, the lithium has a few more, but basically the pair keep me functioning as a sane human being, at least most of the time. And I can't help feeling that anything that works so effec-tively, that's so transformative, has got to be hurting me at another end, maybe sometime further down the road.

I can just hear the words *inoperable brain cancer* being whispered to me by some physician twenty years from now.

I mean, the law of conservation says that no matter or energy is ever destroyed, it's only converted into something else, and I still can't say exactly how my depression has metamorphosed. My guess is it's still hanging out in my head, doing deadly things to my gray mat-ter, or worse, that it's just waiting for the clock on this Prozac stuff to run out so that it can attack again, send me back into a state of cata-tonia, just like those characters in the movie *Awakenings* who fall back into their pre-L-dopa stupor after just a few months.

Reassurance or Dismissal?

Every time I come in for an appointment, I run my misgivings by Dr. Ira. I say something like: Come on, level with me, anything that works this well has got to have some unknown downside.

Or, taking another tack: Look, let's face it, I was one of the first people to be put on Prozac after the FDA approved it. Who's to say that I won't be the test case that proves it causes, well, um, say—*inoperable brain cancer?*

He says a bunch of reassuring things, explains over and over again how carefully he is monitoring me—all the while admitting that psychopharmacology is more art than science, that he and his colleagues are all basically shooting in the dark. And he acts as if a million doctors didn't say the same things to women about DES, about the IUD, about silicone breast implants, as if they didn't once claim that Valium was a nonaddictive tranquilizer and that Halcion was a miracle sleeping pill. As if class-action suits against pharmaceutical companies were not fairly routine by now.

Just the same, I am leaving for Miami Beach the next day, am sufficiently sick of being miserable that I take two little green and white Prozac capsules when I leave his office, and dutifully resume taking a twice-daily dose of lithium, also downing twenty milligrams of Inderal each day—a beta-blocker normally used to lower blood pressure—because I need it to counteract the hand shaking and the other tremorous side effects of lithium. Taking drugs breeds taking more drugs.

And I can't believe, looking at myself in the mirror, seeing what to all eyes must appear to be a young and healthy twenty-five-year-old with flushed skin and visible biceps—I can't believe anyone in his right mind would deny that these are just too damn many pills.

ANATOMY OF MELANCHOLY

Andrew Solomon

Andrew Solomon is a novelist who suffers from clinical depression. In the following selection, he writes about his descent into a debilitating depressive state. Although he had recently gone through a difficult time, Solomon explains, his life seemed to be improving until he was suddenly and inexplicably seized by severe depression. He describes how he endured the low points of the illness, struggling to maintain his sense of self while unable to cope with the business of daily life. His father and close relatives played a crucial role in his recovery, Solomon notes, and medication also helped him to regain his mental balance. However, he points out, the sense that something irreparable has occurred during those months of desperation remains.

I did not experience depression until I had pretty much solved my problems. I had come to terms with my mother's death three years earlier, was publishing my first novel, was getting along with my family, had emerged intact from a powerful two-year relationship, had bought a beautiful new house, was writing well. It was when life was finally in order that depression came slinking in and spoiled everything. I'd felt acutely that there was no excuse for it under the circumstances, despite perennial existential crises, the forgotten sorrows of a distant childhood, slight wrongs done to people now dead, the truth that I am not Tolstoy, the absence in this world of perfect love, and those impulses of greed and uncharitableness which lie too close to the heart—that sort of thing. But now, as I ran through this inventory, I believed that my depression was not only a rational state but also an incurable one. I kept redating the beginning of the depression: since my breakup with my girlfriend, the past October; since my mother's death; since the beginning of her two-year illness; since puberty; since birth. Soon I couldn't remember what pleasurable moods had been like.

I was not surprised later when I came across research showing that the particular kind of depression I had undergone has a higher morbidity rate than heart disease or any cancer. According to a recent study by researchers at Harvard and the World Health Organization, only respiratory infections, diarrhea, and newborn infections cost more years of useful life than major depression. It is projected that by the year 2020 depression could claim more years than war and AIDS put together. And its incidence is rising fast. Between six and ten per cent of all Americans now living are battling some form of this illness; one study indicates that nearly fifty per cent have experienced at least one psychiatric disorder in their lifetime. Treatments are proliferating, but only twenty-eight per cent of all people who have a major depression seek help from a specialist; fifteen per cent of hospitalized patients succeed in killing themselves. Attempting to understand this strange malady, I plunged into intensive research shortly after my recovery. I started by attempting a coherent narrative of my own experience.

Numbness Sets In

In June, 1994, I began to be constantly bored. My first novel had recently been published in England, and yet its favorable reception did little for me. I read the reviews indifferently and felt tired all the time. In July, back home in downtown New York, I found myself burdened by phone calls, social events, conversation. The subway proved intolerable. In August, I started to feel numb. I didn't care about work, family, or friends. My writing slowed, then stopped. My usually headstrong libido evaporated.

All this made me feel that I was losing my self. Scared, I tried to schedule pleasures. I went to parties and failed to have fun, saw friends and failed to connect; I bought things I had previously wanted and gained no satisfaction from them. I was overwhelmed by messages on my answering machine and ceased to return calls. When I drove at night, I constantly thought I was going to swerve into another car. Suddenly feeling I'd forgotten how to use the steering wheel, I would pull over in a sweat.

In September, I had agonizing kidney stones. After a brief hospitalization, I spent a vagabond week migrating from friend to friend. I would stay in the house all day, avoiding the street, and was careful never to go far from the phone. When they came home, I would cry. Sleeping pills got me through the night, but morning began to seem increasingly difficult. From then on, the slippage was steady. I worked even less well, cancelled more plans. I began eating irregularly, seldom feeling hungry. A psychoanalyst I was seeing told me, as I sank lower, that avoiding medication was very courageous.

Seized by Terror

At about this time, night terrors began. My book was coming out in the United States, and a friend threw a party on October 11th. I was feeling too lack-lustre to invite many people, was too tired to stand up much during the party, and sweated horribly all night. The event lives in my mind in ghostly outlines and washed-out colors. When I got home, terror seized me. I lay in bed, not sleeping and hugging my pillow for comfort. Two weeks later—the day before my thirty-first birthday—I left the house once, to buy groceries; petrified for no reason, I suddenly lost bowel control and soiled myself. I ran home, shaking, and went to bed, but I did not sleep, and could not get up the following day. I wanted to call people to cancel birthday plans, but I couldn't. I lay very still and thought about speaking, trying to figure out how. I moved my tongue, but there were no sounds. I had forgotten how to talk. Then I began to cry without tears. I was on my back. I wanted to turn over, but couldn't remember how to do that, either. I guessed that perhaps I'd had a stroke. At about three that afternoon, I managed to get up and go to the bathroom. I returned to bed shivering. Fortunately, my father, who lived uptown, called about then. "Cancel tonight," I said, struggling with the strange words. "What's wrong?" he kept asking, but I didn't know.

If you trip or slip, there is a moment, before your hand shoots out to break your fall, when you feel the earth rushing up at you and you cannot help yourself—a passing, fraction-of-a-second horror. I felt that way hour after hour. Freud once described pleasure as the release of tension; I felt as though I had a physical need, of impossible urgency and discomfort, from which there was no release—as though I were constantly vomiting but had no mouth. My vision began to close. It was like trying to watch TV through terrible static, where you can't distinguish faces, where nothing has edges. The air, too, seemed thick and resistant, as though it were full of mushed-up bread.

Outside Intervention

My father came to my apartment with my brother, his fiancée, and a friend; fortunately, they had keys. I had had nothing to eat in almost two days, and they tried to give me smoked salmon. I ate a bite, then threw up all over myself. The next day, my father took me to my analyst's office. "I need medication," I said, diving deep for the words. "I'm sorry," she said, and she called a psychopharmacologist.

Dr. Alfred Wiener agreed to see me in an hour. He seems to have come out of some "Spellbound"-era shrink movie: he is in his late sixties, smokes cigars, has a European accent, and wears carpet slippers. He has elegant manners and a kindly smile. He asked me a string of specific questions. "Very classic indeed," he said calmly as I trotted out my atrocities. "Don't worry, we'll soon have you well." He wrote a prescription for Xanax, then handed me some Zoloft. "You'll come back tomorrow," he said. "The Zoloft will take some time. The Xanax will alleviate anxiety almost immediately. Don't worry, you have a very normal group of symptoms.". . .

The day after my birthday, I moved to my father's. I was hardly able to get up for the next week. The days were like this: I would wake up panicked. Xanax would relieve the panic if I took enough, but then I would collapse into thick, confusing, dream-heavy sleep. I wanted only to take enough to sleep forever. Whenever I woke up, I took more pills. Killing myself, like taking a shower, was too elaborate an agenda to entertain. All I wanted was for it to stop, but I could not say what "it" was. Words, with which I have always been intimate, seemed suddenly like complex metaphors, the use of which entailed much more energy than I had.

Losing Perspective

Little has been written about the fact that depression is ridiculous. I can remember lying frozen in bed, crying because I was too frightened to take a shower and at the same time knowing that showers are not scary. I ran through the individual steps in my mind: You sit up, turn and put your feet on the floor, stand, walk to the bathroom, open the bathroom door, go to the edge of the tub . . . I divided it into fourteen steps as onerous as the Stations of the Cross. I knew that for years I had taken a shower every day. Hoping that someone else could open the bathroom door, I would, with all the force in my body, sit up; turn and put my feet on the floor; and then feel so incapacitated and frightened that I would roll over and lie face down. I would cry again, weeping because the fact that I could not do it seemed so idiotic to me. At other times, I have enjoyed skydiving: it is easier to climb along a strut toward the tip of a plane's wing against an eighty-mile-an-hour wind at five thousand feet than it was to get out of bed those days.

Evenings, I was able to rise. Most depression has a diurnal rhythm, improving over the course of the day and descending overnight. I could sit up for dinner with my father. I could speak by then. I tried to explain; my father implacably assured me that it would pass, and told me to eat. When I was defeated by the difficulty of getting a piece of lamb chop onto my fork, he would do it for me. He would say he remembered feeding me when I was a child, and would make me promise, jesting, to cut up his lamb chops when he was old and tooth-less. "I used to work twelve hours, go to four parties in an evening," I would say. He would assure me that I would be able to do it all again soon. He could just as well have told me that I would soon be able to build a helicopter of cookie dough and fly to Neptune, so clear was it to me that my real life was definitively over. After dinner, I would return some calls. It is embarrassing to admit depression; to all but my closest friends I said that I'd developed an "obscure tropical virus."

When you are depressed, the past and the future are absorbed entirely by the present, as in the world of a three-year-old. You can neither remember feeling better nor imagine that you will feel better. Being upset, even profoundly upset, is a temporal experience, whereas depression is atemporal. Depression means that you have no point of view. . . .

The Burden of Activity

Inconveniently, I had a reading tour to do after that birthday, and antidepressants usually take about a month to kick in. Still, I was determined to get through it, because I believed that, meds or no meds, if I started giving up on things I would give up on everything and die. Before the first reading, in New York, I spent four hours taking a bath, and then a friend helped me take a cold shower, and then I went and read. I felt as though I had baby powder in my mouth, and I couldn't hear very well, and I kept thinking I might faint, but I did it. Then I went to bed for three days. Though I could keep the tension under control if I took enough Xanax, I still found mundane activities nearly impossible. I woke up every day in a panic, early, and needed a few hours to conquer my fear before getting out of bed. But I could force myself out in public for an hour or two in the evening.

I had thought I could not possibly go to California for a reading the next week. My father took me there: he got me on and off the plane and to the hotel. So drugged up that I was almost asleep, I could manage these changes, which would have been inconceivable a week earlier. I knew that the more I managed to do, the less I would want to die. During my first dinner in San Francisco, I suddenly felt my depression lift. I chose my own food. I had been spending days on end with my father, but I had no idea what had been happening in his life, except me; depression is a disease of self-obsession. We talked that night as though we were catching up after months apart. When I finally went to bed, I was almost ecstatic. I had some chocolates from my mini-bar, wrote a letter. I felt ready for the world.

The next morning, I felt just as bad as I had ever felt. My father helped me get out of bed and turned on the shower. He tried to get me to eat, but I was too frightened to chew. I managed to drink some milk. These days, a quarter of a milligram of Xanax will put me to sleep for eight hours. That day, I took seven milligrams of Xanax and was still so tense I couldn't sit still. Dr. Wiener had by then started me on Navane, an antipsychotic drug that we hoped would allow me to take the Xanax less often. (I was then taking it every forty-five minutes or so, and in higher doses at bedtime.) The perpetual sensation of tension was completely exhausting, and the cumulative sedative effects of the Xanax and the Navane began to overwhelm me.

Prostrate and Helpless

The third week of my tour, I lost the ability to remain upright for very long. I would walk for a few minutes and then I would have to lie down. I could no more control that need than I could the need to breathe. At my readings, I would cling to the podium. I would start skipping paragraphs to get through. When I was done, I would sit in a chair and hold on to the seat. As soon as I could leave the room, on any excuse, I would lie down again, often on a bathroom floor. I remember going for a walk with a friend outside Berkeley, hoping that nature might do me good. I had not left my bed for the previous fifty-eight hours; because I'd reduced my Xanax substantially, I was beginning to experience high anxiety again. We got out of my friend's car and walked for almost fifteen minutes, and then I couldn't go any farther. I lay down, fully dressed in nice clothes, in the mud. "Please let me stay here," I said, and I didn't care about standing up ever again. For an hour I lay in that mud, feeling the water seep through, and then my friend pretty much carried me back to the car. Those same nerves that had been scraped raw now seemed to be wrapped in lead.

During my reading tour, I took a lot of cold showers, which got me through the necessary hours. As soon as I could drag myself out of bed, I'd do exercises or, if I could manage it, I'd go to a gym. I felt as though the exercise filtered the depression out of my blood, helped me to get cleaner. "Most people feel that," Norman Rosenthal, at the National Institute of Mental Health (N.I.M.H.), says. "It's very strong anecdotally."

In the end, I cancelled only one reading. Between November 1st and December 15th, I visited eleven cities. Doing those readings was the most difficult endeavor of my life. My publisher's publicist, who had organized my reading tour, came with me for more than half of it, cheering me through; my father came with me the rest of the time, and when we were apart he called me every few hours. I was never alone for long. The knowledge that I was loved was not in itself a cure, but without it I would not have been able to complete the tour. I would have found a place to lie down in the woods and I would have stayed there until I froze and died. Recovery depends enormously on support. The depressives I've met who have done the best were cushioned with love. Nothing taught me more about the love of my father and my friends than my own depression. . . .

An Ongoing Battle

On the happy day when we lose depression, we will lose a great deal with it. As the sun seems brighter and clearer when it comes on a rare day of English summer after ten months of gray skies than it can ever seem in the tropics, so recent happiness feels enormous and embracing and beyond anything I have ever imagined. In the course of my depression, I reached a strange point at which I could not see the line between my own tendency to theatricality and the reality of my illness. The line is still not clear, but there is someone or something here writing these words, a unionist me that held on until the rebel chemicals had been brought back into line. Some ropy fibre holds fast even when most of the self has been stripped from it; we know what chemistry is and how deep it runs, and yet anyone who lives through this knows that the shifting self reaches beyond serotonin and dopamine. I'm more confident, in some odd way, than I've ever imagined being. I do not think that I will ever again try to kill myself, nor do I think that I would give my life up readily if my plane crashed in a desert. I would struggle tooth and nail to survive. The opposite of depression is not happiness but vitality, and my life, as I write this, is vital, even when it's sad. I may wake up sometime next year without my mind again. But I know what is left of me when my mind is gone and my body is going. I was not brought up religious, and think that when you die you're dead, yet I have also discovered what I guess I would have to call a soul—something I had never imagined until one day . . . when Hell came to pay me a surprise visit. It's a precious discovery. This week, on a chilly night when I was overtired, I felt a momentary flash of hopelessness, and wondered, as I so often do, whether I was slipping; for a petrifying instant, a lightning-quick flash, I wanted a car to run me over, and I had to clench my teeth to stay on the sidewalk until the light turned green. Nevertheless, I cannot find it in me to regret entirely the course my life took.

THE BEAST: A RECKONING WITH DEPRESSION

Tracy Thompson

Tracy Thompson is a reporter for the *Washington Post* and the author of *The Beast: A Reckoning with Depression*, from which the following selection is taken. Thompson writes that depression has haunted her since her childhood; she even named the disorder "The Beast". In 1992, two years after she began an effective drug treatment, Thompson decided to write an article about her struggle with depression for the *Washington Post*. Although she was nervous about presenting her own history to millions of readers, she received an overwhelmingly positive response and was able, through her article, to help many other people.

My body aches intermittently, in waves, as if I had malaria. I eat with no appetite, simply because the taste of food is one of my dwindling number of pleasures. I am tired, so tired. Last night I lay like a pile of old clothes, and when David came to bed I did not stir. Sex is a foreign notion. At work today I am forgetful; I have trouble forming sentences, I lose track of them halfway through, and my words keep getting tangled. I look at my list of things to do today, and keep on looking at it; nothing seems to be happening. Things seem sad to me. This morning I thought of the woman who used to live in my old house, who told me she went to Sears to buy fake lace curtains. It seemed a forlorn act—having to save your pennies, not being able to afford genuine lace. (Why? a voice in my head asks. The curtains she bought looked perfectly nice.) I feel as if my brain were a lump of protoplasm with tiny circuits embedded in it, and some of the wires keep shorting out. There are tiny little electrical fires up there, leaving crispy sections of neurons smoking and ruined.

At lease that's how it seems. Sitting in the subway station, waiting for the train, I realize I am not thinking straight, so I do what I've done before in this situation: I get out a pen and paper and start writing down what I call my "dysfunctional thoughts." Just between the car and the subway station escalator, I accumulate these: "Everybody but me is in shape. I am fat." Then: "My career is going nowhere. I'm never going to get a promotion at work. They think I'm second-rate." And: "My relationship with David is not working. I'm getting irritable and withdrawn, finding fault. More proof that I can't handle intimacy."

Writing these down doesn't help immediately, as I knew it wouldn't, but I file them away for future reference. I take it on faith that I am thinking in distorted ways at the moment. But I'm never really sure of that when it would most help to know. I don't even know when this current siege began—a week ago? A month ago? The onset is so gradual, and these things are hard to tell. All I know is, the Beast is back.

The Force of Depression

It is called depression, and my experiences with it have shaped my life—altered my personality, affected my most intimate relationships, changed the course of my career—in ways I will probably never be fully aware of. These days, however, the Beast has been cornered—which is to say that he escapes from time to time, but I have some control over him. I have an array of new antidepressant drugs at my disposal—far more powerful than traditional antidepressants, faster-acting and with fewer side effects—and a psychiatrist with whom I have developed trust and a good working relationship. After many years of pretending the Beast did not exist, I now have deep respect for my adversary.

I call him "Beast" because it suits him—though I imagine "him" not as a creature but as a force, something that has slipped outside the bounds of natural existence, a psychic freight train of roaring despair. For most of my life, the Beast has been my implacable and unpredictable enemy, disappearing for months or years, then returning in strength. He appeared in the most benign of guises, hiding in plain view behind a word I thought I understood, but didn't. I was using the word "depression" as early as fourteen in my diary, but I did so in the nonmedical sense of the word—the ordinary, transient despair of being a teenager. Yet, even in grammar school, there were long stretches—weeks, maybe months, it is impossible now to say—when every morning I counted the hours that had to pass before I could crawl into bed again, times when I escaped to the shower and turned on the water full blast to disguise the sound of my weeping, unhappy over something I could not name. I suspected something was wrong with me, that this flat and colorless world I lived in was different from the one most other people lived in, and I wanted desperately to be "normal." At the same time, I had no real assurance this was not normal. "Everybody gets lonely sometimes," my mother told me, when I tried to tell her what it was like. How could she help me? I had no words to describe this thing. And she suffered from depression too.

And so, very early, I began to try to understand.

I trace the beginnings of that endeavor back to a winter afternoon when I was fourteen, sitting in my bedroom in a suburb of Atlanta. In my lap was a blank green stenographer's pad; in my hand was a pen. I know the precise date, because it's recorded there in my careful schoolgirl penmanship: December 29, 1969. I was beginning a private journal and, I wrote, I had two reasons for trying this experiment. One was to practice my writing. The other purpose was "to put down the cause of my depressions and to see if I can help myself that way. . . . It sounds horrible, and it is, but a couple of times I have thought how nice it would be to kill myself!!!"

As time went by, depression became more than just a personal struggle, but also a subject on which I could practice my writer's craft, even in those long years when I did not know what I was describing. It seemed natural to become a journalist—an occupation hospitable to persons with mood disorders. Having a mood disorder is not synonymous with having artistic talent, but it is true that people in the so-called creative professions—writers, actors, artists, musicians—have a higher than normal incidence of such illnesses, and there are also a disproportionate number of alcoholics in these fields whose drinking may be an attempt to medicate the anxiety of depression. I didn't know this when I was twenty-one, the year I became a newspaper reporter. I just knew I loved newspapers. Mostly, I loved the people who wrote for them: the hard-bitten colleagues who chortled over the dead stripper whose will directed the undertaker to put a whip and a jar of peanut butter in her coffin ("What for?" I asked, and they guffawed), but who turned to mush over a story about a child lost in the woods. I wanted, of course, to write brilliant fiction—but real life kept intervening. It was so much more interesting. I watched and noted, and what I saw and felt went into my journal. It was an adolescent undertaking, still; every incident was invested with high drama in those pages, and hardly a day went by when I did not note my psychic temperature. It would be years before I developed an interest in brain biology, before I would be able to see the story I was researching as bigger than myself. But those scraps of raw material would prove useful later, when I searched them for patterns. I was, as they say in the newspaper trade, "saving string."

Spreading the News

In 1992, two years after I began to get effective drug therapy for my depression, the personal and the professional merged in an article I wrote about my experience for the *Washington Post*. Several colleagues warned me against writing about such a personal subject. They said that revealing I had suffered a mental illness would harm my career, and for a while I held back, afraid they were right. But the more I thought about it, the more I wondered. Suppose they *were* right? Did silence, in the long run, help me? I also felt the inequity of my situation. My colleagues had written first-person accounts of their heart attacks or their gallbladder surgery, if they had learned something of interest, and their stories were considered valuable contributions to public understanding. Depression was surely as common as heart disease or gallbladder surgery; I knew half a dozen people who had endured serious episodes of it, and just as many who had dealt with it in a family member. They did not talk about it freely, however. Some of my colleagues at the *Post* knew that I had been hospitalized for depression, but they tended to bring the subject up in stairwells, or at private lunches. Over and over, I was struck by the way in which each person categorized his or her experience as unique. *It wasn't really "depression," it was stress.* Or, *I never spread it around, but my father was hospitalized for six months; we thought he'd never get better.* Or, *Nobody in my family has ever seen a psychiatrist, I'm the oddball.* After a while, it seemed logical to suppose that there were a great many people who had some experience with this illness.

There were. By nine a.m. on the Tuesday morning my article appeared, my direct line at the office had recorded a little over forty voice mail messages, not counting calls coming in to other parts of the paper. The pace of calls continued all week. For many readers, it was the first news that their pain was, in fact, a medical problem and not a character weakness, that a great many "high achievers" suffered the debilitating effects of depressive episodes and in the intervals still managed to pursue demanding careers—and that help was available. Like me, they had suspected that something was fundamentally wrong with how they felt. But they had gotten stuck at the last conceptual hurdle—which was to say, out loud, "I have a mental illness." Many expressed immense relief; it was as if a familiar word—"depression"—had suddenly become three-dimensional, revealing the adversary behind its ordinary facade. One caller comes vividly to mind. "I'm Peggy," she said. The call was logged early Tuesday morning; she must have just read the paper. She was weeping. "I read your story. I think you may have just saved my life."

After four days of this, overwhelmed with the reaction I had unleashed in myself and others, I went home and, for a little while, pulled the bedcovers over my head.

Studying the Self

I emerged, eventually, with the idea of writing about this illness in a new way—not as a memoir of insanity, but as the chronicle of a time I have lived through. To me, it's an era which began on that winter afternoon in 1969 in Atlanta, in a time and place in which people talked vaguely about "nervous breakdowns" and "female trouble," and which continues to the present, when many laymen can converse with some sophistication about disorders of neurotransmitters in the brain. My task would be to subject myself to the same scrutiny I applied when I wrote about other people, to write about an intensely personal subject in the most objective way I could. I would try to apply the tools of journalism—the ability to note significant details and ask the right questions, the dogged pursuit of a pattern of meaning in a jumble of facts—to the art of personal history. I would try to pass through the mirror of self and describe what I saw from the other side.

This is an interesting concept. The brain is the only organ that tries to make sense of its pain. It is as if the bone were trying to understand the break, as if the blood vessel could comprehend its rupture. But this is also its greatest impediment to understanding. The mind clings fiercely to any alternative to chaos, even if that alternative is self-destruction; the tunnel vision of suicide, when death seems the only solution to an intolerable existence, is the brain's categorical rejection of the preposterous notion that anything about its perception of events might be amiss. But the reverse ought also to be true: the healthy mind might be able to understand its own malfunction.

The array of symptoms we call depression is a territory ventured into many times over the centuries, each time by explorers fascinated by different elements of its topography. It seems to us a twentieth-century phenomenon, but in fact, it is an old and well-documented illness. Greek physicians in the time of Hippocrates described a mental condition involving prolonged and inexplicable feelings of fear and anxiety, which they ascribed to an excess of "black bile." The Greek term for that—*melaina chole*—is the root of the English word "melancholy." In the fourteenth century, it was known as "melancholia," which reflected the sadness that is another dominant feature; in the nineteenth century, it had become "neurasthenia," with its hysterical connotations of swooning fits and vague physical malaise. The word "depression," used in a clinical sense, did not come into common usage until the twentieth century, and already it has passed back into the domain of the layman. Today, as we struggle to put all the pieces of the picture into a single frame, the most common medical term is "affective disorder." That, and other modern locutions such as "neurobiological disorder," may be more clinically precise, but they lack the music of some words from earlier centuries. So far, nothing has quite worked; we still lack a distinctive and accurate name for this ancient shadow on the brain.

Depression in a Social Context

Depression meets with a particularly ambivalent reception in modern America. Our frontier ethic of self-sufficiency has evolved into a modern taste for self-absorption and the inverted quest for status found in victimhood. When it comes to depression, Americans tend either to remain stoic and blind to the most flagrant symptoms, or to adopt the role of wounded children whose problems are entirely the fault of forces beyond their control—a bad upbringing, societal ills, or rotten genes. Sometimes it seems as if the most widely heard spokesmen on this issue are divided into two camps: those who believe depression isn't truly an illness at all, and those whose lives have been one long tragic experience with nothing but depression.

Despite our recent preoccupation with psychopharmacology, depression is a complex illness of both internal and external origins, the interaction of nature and nurture. That makes it all the harder to define and our inability to do so may explain why even the most generous medical insurance plans limit coverage for this illness. Yet according to a recent estimate in *the Journal of Clinical Psychiatry*, depression accounts for a $43.7-billion-per-year burden on the American economy, measured in medical costs, lost productivity, and the lost economic contributions of wage earners who die young from depression-related suicide. For American business, depression is the ne'er-do-well relative suspected of skimming money from the cash register; employers ignore or condescend to him, hoping that one day he will just go away. But he won't.

These days, any good bookstore has shelves of books about mood disorders, many of them medically sophisticated, some of the level of pop psychology, and much in between. In cyberspace, people swap questions about medication and coping hints via files with names like "Depression Chatline." Judging from the number of entries, interest in this subject ranks up there with that old standby, "relationships." The pharmacist in my neighborhood in Washington, D.C., jokes about how he should order Prozac by the truckload, since everybody in the neighborhood is taking it.

But, he adds, not everybody wants to personally own up to that.

Shame and Secrecy

His words point out the aspect people don't talk about: even in this avalanche of information, the stigma remains. I know of one highly regarded reporter for the *New York Times* who pays his own psychiatric bills, fearful that submitting them to the company health insurance plan will stymie his career. He may be right; in any event, the *Times'* mental health coverage is not generous, so he's not missing out on much. A young White House aide, recruited straight from college because of his obvious intelligence and potential, tells me over lunch how he sneaks out of the office to see his psychiatrist, how he worries that the side effects of his medication will become evident to his co-workers. As my illness has done so many times in the past, his is producing such anxiety that to simply complete a thought is an excruciating task, and writing a complete paragraph can take an entire morning. It is a debilitating state to be in, all the more so in Washington, a city with no time for the slow-witted. Depression robs the mind of its normal power to concentrate and analyze. From the outside, looking at apparently healthy people hiding their depression, the deficits are subtle and easily missed. But to the sufferer, they are as devastating as if a knitting needle had sliced 20 IQ points from his frontal lobe while he slept. This is what the White House aide tells me over lunch, though he doesn't need to. He is in such pain it is palpable, so brittle I think he might shatter before my eyes. He is very sick, and so very ashamed.

I understand his shame; I've felt it myself. Sometimes I still do. To those who have never experienced depression, this must be an infuriating illness—easy to fake, quite possible to conceal, hard to distinguish at times from whining and simple malingering. That frustration no doubt explains some of the treatments for depression, which over the centuries have included emetics, purges, cold showers, or prescriptions for "mother's little helper" pills, all dispensed with a kind of weary tolerance. I sometimes wonder how much this all too human reaction of frustration has to do with the advice of a few doctors who in recent years have opposed the use of psychoactive drugs altogether—and whether any of them would ever think of telling a diabetic patient to try harder to get well.

The stigma of depression is sometimes unwittingly perpetrated by those of us who write about it, who subscribe to the notion that having a mood disorder makes one "special." Many first-person accounts of depression contain a hopelessly compromised message: it is wrong, those writers say, to attach a stigma to an illness which is a medical problem like any other . . . except that it *is* different, since only artists suffer. This is an elitist view. Grocery store clerks and bus drivers also suffer, but lack the leisure to write about it. And it is a view which ignores some unattractive truths, including the fact that depression tends to foster an array of personality traits which can remain as its permanent legacy: manipulative behavior, passivity, unremitting self-absorption.

I do not believe depression is the special province of any particular group; I don't see it as a "feminist" issue. I am distrustful of data which show that the incidence of depression is much higher among women than among men, because I do not think our culture has ever permitted men to express psychic pain the same ways that women do. Nor can we know with any degree of certainty how the statistics in our century stand in comparison to, say, the incidence of depression in late-nineteenth-century France. Statistics on depression are like statistics about crime; all we know is the reported incidence. They give us broad landmarks, not precise information.

It is one of the ironies of the history of this illness that new drug treatments for it—drugs with names like Prozac, Paxil and Zoloft—emerged in this country about the same time the antidrug crusade reached its zenith. The antidrug slogans are everywhere, emblazoned on shopping bags and on the sides of tractor trailer trucks. "Drugs are a dead end." "Just say no to drugs." "Drugs kill." Hardly any school in the country does not have a sign proudly announcing that it is a "drug-free zone." Added to this is the belief among many non-M.D. psychotherapists that drugs are an illicit shortcut, that the only way to truly solve problems is through years of painful self-analysis. "I'm a little scared of Prozac," one prominent Washington psychotherapist told me at a party once. "I prefer to treat the whole person"—as if, I thought, she somehow understood the brain to be completely unrelated to, say, the colon or the pancreas.

But she's right, in a way. Ray Fuller, one of the Eli Lilly scientists who developed Prozac, put it this way when I interviewed him for a *Washington Post story* several years ago: "If the brain were simple enough for us to understand, we would be too simple to understand it." Altering brain chemistry alters behavior, he said—but the hidden reverse is also true: altering behavior alters brain chemistry. This makes sense to me. And in accepting this, I find no diminishment of the mystery of human consciousness. If anything, the mystery deepens.

A Journey to Better Understanding

Mental illness is a kind of exile into a foreign territory of the mind, although this foreign territory is right next door. It is a room—imagine it as plain white, featureless, empty—which most people may not enter, and from which others may never leave. Those of us who have seen it from the inside may or may not be able to send back bulletins, and until now those bulletins have been understandable to others only in the music of poetry, in music itself, or in the simplest of prose.

"It's cold in here," we may say. "I hurt. I am miserable."

And those on the other side may hear. They may even partly understand. But the message has never come through in clear, everyday language, told with coherence, sophistication, and detail.

Until now, that is. Now that medicine has come up with effective ways to treat depression, those of us who suffer from it have become co-investigators into this new science of the brain; for the first time, sizable numbers of us can return from that featureless white room to add our voices to the debate about psychotropic drugs and their place in society. It's a discussion which, so far, has mostly excluded us, though it shouldn't; no one outranks the patient as an authority on what is happening inside his own head. We are also under an increasing obligation to confront our illness, seek the proper treatment, and to the extent we can, begin the work of changing the behaviors fostered by depression. This is not blaming the victim; it is—to use a trendy phrase—empowering the victim. To fail at this, to surrender to the devouring self-pity this illness can engender, violates an unwritten law of society, which needs all the talents and energies of every member. To remain a victim of depression when I have been given the tools to be healthy, or at least healthier, means that I am withholding a part of me from people who might need whatever I have to give.

Looking back at those carefully rounded letters in the green stenographer's pad, I marvel at how little that fourteen-year-old knew, and how prescient those words were in describing the struggle she faced. And I'm glad she made it.

THE LEGACY OF DEPRESSION

Martha Manning

In the following selection, Martha Manning describes not just her own experiences with depression but also those of other family members. Manning writes that she wanted to understand why and how depression had struck generations of her family. She explains that the legacy of depression in her immediate family has skipped generations: She and her grandmother were both afflicted by depression, but her mother and her daughter were not. In addition, she examines the resonating power that close familial relationships can have on a person, well after daily interaction has ceased. Manning is a therapist and the author of *Undercurrents: A Life Beneath the Surface*.

My family is haunted by depression. My mother can trace it back in her family at least six generations and it's in my father's family, too. When it hits, it hits hard. We don't get "down in the dumps," we get lost in the pits. Some people find themselves or are found, others get lost forever. The melancholies, nerves and breakdowns of my ancestors landed them in sanitariums, rest homes or in upstairs rooms from which they never emerged. Treatment involved the state-of-the-art interventions of the time—cold packs, electric current, sedating drugs. Sometimes people got better. Sometimes they didn't.

Six months into my own treatment for an episode of depression that scared me in its speed, severity and stubbornness, I had placed most of my emotional cards on the table, but was disappointed that my therapist still hadn't constructed some brilliant framework in which my difficulties and those of my family could be finally uncovered and our dysfunction excised. Since he never volunteered his opinion on the subject, I finally just demanded, "Why are there so many problems in my family?" He shrugged and replied calmly, "Because there are so many people in it."

My first reaction was, "I'm paying $100 an hour for this?" And yet, years later, his comment still stands firm among my list of top 10 therapeutic interventions of all time. The poet Mary Karr, author of the celebrated *Liars' Club*, a memoir of a colorful and tremendously chaotic family, recently echoed my therapist's comment when she

From Martha Manning, "The Legacy." This article first appeared in the *Family Therapy Networker* (January/February 1997) and is reprinted here with permission.

wrote that her definition of a dysfunctional family is "a family with more than one person in it."

Theory and Life

My therapist's comment looks naive sandwiched between some of the more elaborate observations other therapists and clinical supervisors have made to me over the years. But in addition to comforting me with its common sense about the variety of ways families suffer, his words have been an insistent caution whenever I am seduced too quickly into facile interpretations of psychopathology. There is, after all, a very thin line between theoretical elegance and bullshit. These days, the easier the explanation of something as complicated as the relationship between families and depression, the less I trust it.

For every connection we find between our favorite theories and what we see in our consulting rooms, there are probably a hundred such families whose members somehow muddle through in defiance of our ideas about how dysfunctional they and their families are. Understanding the legacy of depression in a family requires more than genetic mapping, family diagrams, or symptom checklists. Each of us is the product of a complex weaving of genes and expectations, biochemistry and family myths, and the configuration of our family's strengths, as well as its vulnerabilities. To truly appreciate the complexity of the weave, we have to sort out the contributions of individual threads to the overall design. Yet, in describing a weaving it would be ridiculous to say, "Well, there's a red thread and over there is a blue thread and here's a gold thread." While these separate observations yield *pieces* of information, they provide no overall view of the fabric. It is only when we see how red threads braided with blue threads influence the pattern in particular ways that we can even begin to grasp the design of the whole.

Memories of Grandmother

My own memory of being haunted by depression extends back to my great-grandmother who lived into her nineties and died when I was about 10. As I began to put things together about the relationship between my grandmother and her mother, I started to wonder whether the dulling of self I sometimes experienced, and its power to contaminate energy and joy, played leap frog with the generations—hopping over my great-grandmother and landing on my grandmother, leaping over my mother and crashing down on me.

My great-grandmother was either authoritative or controlling, depending on how negatively her behavior was affecting you at the time. When we made our annual family visit to my grandmother in Massachusetts, we knew our visit would include a pilgrimage to her mother, Grammy Hale. As young as 6 or 7, I knew that there was a whole lot more going on during those visits than I could grasp. My intuitions were confirmed whenever children were dismissed immediately following raised voices. I sensed something big happened during those dismissals. Something bad. Later I found out that these were the times my great-grandmother roundly castigated my grandmother. It didn't matter for what. It could have been my grandmother's break away from a middle-class Irish Catholic neighborhood after her marriage to reside in a big house on the Waspiest street in the town. Or it could have been the tone of a brief comment my grandmother had made weeks before. The crime didn't matter. The punishment was always the same: my great-grandmother's total and complete disgust.

After each visit, as we drove back from Salem, I noticed the way my grandmother deflated, remaining silent on the way back to her house. She was almost impossible to distract from her brooding, even with our most entertaining attempts. Even when we arrived back to her wonderful beach house and celebrated our freedom from creaking musty homes and strange old women, my grandmother was elusive She stayed in her room, shades drawn against the sun and the ocean, windows shut tight against the clean salt air. It frustrated me to think that she was making herself oblivious to the most obvious ways to feel better.

Another Side Revealed

When we kids asked what was wrong with Grandmother, grown-ups always told us the same things. Grandmother was "tired," Grandmother "needed some rest," Grandmother "wasn't well" And we were told that the only thing we could possibly do to make her feel better was nearly impossible: "Be quiet." Trays that were delivered to her room earlier in the day were retrieved untouched. She didn't even want to see me, her "golden girl" who could usually snap her out of anything. Sometimes, I'd sneak into her room and lie next to her when she was sleeping, matching my breathing to hers and stroking her hair and face. She didn't have a fever, she wasn't throwing up and I didn't see spots anywhere so she wasn't sick in any way I knew about. I wondered if sadness grew with age and actually made people sick. The reasons each siege of sadness finally ended were no clearer to me than the reasons it began. When I asked about these things, unlike other times when I knew information was intentionally withheld, I almost believed my mother when her smile flickered for a moment and she said she didn't know.

On her good days my grandmother was magic—extravagant, energetic and always interested. She allowed my cousins and me to tag along with her on her many errands and activities. She let us know that we were all perfectly wonderful children, despite our parents' petty complaints about us. She was fun in a way my mother never was. But as I grew older, I learned about the other side. On her bad days, I could see my grandmother wilt before my eyes. There was nowhere to tag along, because she didn't go anywhere. She never got fully dressed and when she did, it wasn't worth it. She didn't laugh. She didn't think I was perfect anymore. The air felt heavy around her, very still and hard to breathe. My grandfather, a C.P.A., seemed always to be working. My grandmother went to bed early (many times before dark). For a woman who spent as much time in bed as she did, I was always puzzled by her daily complaint that she didn't get any sleep. My grandfather recedes in my memory as a major player when my grandmother was nursing her depressions and sulks. It's like he just disappeared at those times.

In early adolescence, my relationship with my grandmother changed. Now I felt some unspoken expectation that with my new maturity, I owed her something. Now she wanted me to listen to her complaints of how badly she slept or how my grandfather worked too much or how her children didn't understand her. I couldn't stand her laments. And, since I couldn't do anything about her complaints, I left each interaction frustrated and resentful. She scared me in a way I couldn't and didn't want to understand. I felt an uneasy resonance with her, a sonar that picked up on cues that predicted a shift in her mood

Mother's Manner

My mother was not magic. She was practical, rational and smart. As a little kid, I knew that and I loved her for it, because to me it meant that she would always take care of me, that no matter what happened, she was a constant. As our personalities diverged, she seemed more formidable. My mother was in control of her feelings. Mine spilled out all over the place. To my mother, the fact that every day was a new day was a good thing. I was never so sure. I also learned that my own dark moods were best kept to myself. As the oldest of six, I, like my mother before me, was praised for being so responsible, so capable at such an early age. I loved the praise, but I hated the reasons for it.

My mother had a no-nonsense approach to unhappiness. Stay busy, think of someone worse off than yourself, offer it up for the souls in Purgatory. At the pediatrician's office when two or three of us lined up with our bare asses vulnerable to imminent medical intervention, one of us invariably burst into loud and contagious tears, protests and screams. I remember more than once my mother leaning over and whispering, "If you *must* cry, cry quietly."

I recall her curiosity and impatience at my unremitting despair following being dumped by a boy when I was 13. She was sympathetic to the pain of such an experience and allowed that there was nothing like a good, cleansing cry. It was the intensity and duration of it that proved problematic. My mother had about 15 minutes in mind, whereas I was planning to make a weekend out of it.

Early on, I considered myself flawed in a way that she wasn't. Unlike my mother, I had difficulty with what she calls "compartmentalizing." She could quickly extricate herself from awful feelings; I became mired in them. By my mid to late teens, I began to struggle with the variability of my moods, something that the steamroller approach to life I had learned from my mother could not control. I wondered which woman, my mother or my grandmother, was the preview of my future. My unspoken fear that increased with age was that I was destined to become my grandmother

A Complex Relationship

I understood more about the nature of my mother's strength when I saw her in the context of my grandmother's vulnerability. As I grew old enough to realize that my mother and I could experience diametrically opposed feelings on the same exact subject, I realized she hated visits to my grandmother—the very same trips I loved. When I was 6, I looked at the calendar and cried out, "Two more days till vacation." My mother's face got as stormy as it ever gets. She clenched her teeth and spit out, "This is many things, but it is definitely *not a vacation*."

When my grandmother's mood changed, my mother's did, too. Upon our annual arrival at my grandparents' beach house, it seemed like my grandmother almost willfully fell backward into helplessness and depression. And, in response, my mother went into overdrive. After feeding her own six kids dinner in our adjoining cottage, she rushed up to the main house to feed my grandparents, who somehow made it through the other 50 weeks of the year just fine.

But cooking was the *least* of my mother's duties. She was my grandmother's personal cheerleader, her therapist, the person who got her up and going, who tried to shift my grandmother's automatic negative outlook at least to neutral. One of my most common memories of those visits is the way my mother and grandmother sat around the kitchen table. My mother always looked like she was sitting on tacks and my grandmother always looked like she was sinking in mud. The sheer exhaustion she conveyed in the act of stirring her tea made it look like she was mixing cement.

Their conversations always stopped short when I walked in the room, but my mother didn't look at all like she looked in the many kitchen-table conversations she shared with her friends. When I became a therapist, I realized that during those times my grandmother and mother were "in session." It was only once we were on our way home again that I could see my mother's shoulders relax. She started smiling again and tolerated our loud and stupid car games

Recurring Patterns

In retrospect, I see how that pattern repeated itself with my therapist-husband when I was depressed, as we sat on the bed or at the table and he tried to get me to articulate what was wrong. Anyone who has ever been seriously depressed knows that that task is as daunting as asking a lame man to tap dance. In addition, it leads to mutual frustration, anger and, ultimately, helplessness. It was only when we both gave up the expectation that my husband could somehow "cure" me that we moved from pseudo therapy to true support. Instead of reaching out with well-intentioned "therapeutic" interventions, he shifted to questions like, "What would help right now?" My therapist was always willing to include Brian in our sessions and, even though they were not present, to recognize Brian and my daughter, Keara, not only as my support system but as people who were suffering also. This freed them from the responsibility of those awful sessions at the kitchen table, where the certainty is that if you stay with this depressed person for one minute longer, you will drown as well.

My grandmother constantly sighed, something my mother never did. It was not an "Oh well" kind of sigh or a "That's life" kind of sigh. Hers was an exhalation that sounded like it could possibly end in her demise. It was a sigh of surrender. But as I got older, I understood that it wasn't pure fatigue or sorrow or hopelessness. It was, in its essence, an angry sigh. It was a challenge: "Just you try and make me feel better. I dare you."

Passing on Disappointment

In my twenties, my mother began to tell me about her childhood. She recalled being very happy until she was a teenager. My grandmother was dynamic—an energetic cleaner and planner. She loved children and was always wonderful with them. But in early adolescence, something changed. My mother began to return from school to a sink full of dirty dishes, her mother in bed for no obvious reason and no dinner planned. "My memory of ninth grade," she told me "is of gritting my teeth and thinking, 'Oh God, now I have that mess to face.'" But my mother did more than face it. She took care of it.

The expectation that she do it and keep on doing it was never articulated. It was assumed and rewarded with abundant praise, which totally hooked my mother in very short order.

As children, we believed all of my grandmother's promises that things would be better "if only"—"If only you lived closer, I'd be happier." "If only your aunt was easier to deal with." "If only your grandfather didn't work so hard." When I was 10, my mother (who rarely said bad things about people) insinuated that we shouldn't count on those extravagant promises our grandmother had made. When we leapt to our poor grandmother's defense, my mother responded, "This is the truth. It's what goes on. I'm giving you the truth. I never got that from my mother. But you will always have it from me."

When I had my own child at the age of 25, my mother became much more open in expressing her frustration—with my grandmother for not changing and with herself for not being able to make her. In my late twenties and thirties, the depressive fog that had shadowed me for a long time grew more difficult to override or outrun.

Depression's Reappearance

I moved to Boston with my husband and daughter to do a postdoctoral fellowship at McLean Hospital. We found a house several miles away from my grandmother, to her great delight. I was thoroughly unhappy with the fellowship, McLean and the move, especially as I realized why my mother had consciously put 500 miles between her mother and herself. It was so sad to see my grandmother's magic destroyed by something so insidious and powerful, that neither my love nor my training could change it. I knew she was in her own hell, yet there were times I wanted to coax her or kick her out of it, dismiss her complaints and sighs, but I couldn't. And I feared I was looking at my future. I didn't want anyone to feel that way about me.

My first cousin—the firstborn in her family of seven—was going through her own hell at the time from depression, a hell that culminated in suicide in her early twenties. My own deepening depression and my cousin's suicide catapulted me into psychotherapy with a psychiatrist referred by my health plan. I told him I was anxious. He told me I was depressed. Yeah, I admitted, I had my moods, but no way was I depressed in the way my cousin or grandmother was. As evidence against his diagnosis, I listed my accomplishments, the many responsibilities I fulfilled. But 30 minutes into my session with him I was convinced that I was indeed depressed. At the end of our first session, he turned to me solemnly and said, "You really believe that life is something to be endured, to be overcome." I looked back at him suspiciously, wondering if it was a trick question "It isn't?" I asked. He told me we had our work cut out for us and scheduled a session for the next week.

Our work in the five months that remained in my fellowship was fairly structured and involved learning ways to manage my anxiety and set limits in the many areas in which I felt overwhelmed. Perhaps the most significant result of the work was that I decided not to accept a job at my fellowship and remain in the Boston area, but to return to Washington to accept an academic position there.

The Shadow

Not long after we moved back, I began to hear my grandmother's sighs in my own labored breathing. I, too, felt the weight of the spoon as I stirred my tea. I knew that making a peanut butter and jelly sandwich should be far less than a 30-minute operation. I entered individual psychotherapy, found it extremely helpful, particularly in quieting the loud voice of perfection that used to rule my expectations of myself, and the panic that had begun to sneak up from behind and immobilize me.

But my depression continued—despite insight, despite a good marriage, despite a child I dearly loved. I finally agreed to try antidepressants and was horrified when my psychiatrist recommended imipramine, the same medicine my grandmother had used in her late seventies, with moderate success, but difficult side effects. My psychiatrist must have registered the horror on my face. He reassured me that he always chooses as the first antidepressant a drug that has worked with other family members.

He was right. The medicine helped quickly and dramatically. It lifted a lifelong weight off my back and made me wonder, "Is this how regular people feel?" But like many people who take psychotropic medications for significant periods of time, I struggled with questions like, "Why can't I do this on my own?" or, looking at the tiny pills, I wondered, "Is this all that stands between hell and me?"

Therapy's Attempts

Fortunately my psychiatrist and I already had a strong therapeutic relationship. Yet despite the benefits of the antidepressant, I still feared that I was destined to be my grandmother, a fear no drug could erase. I didn't want her resignation, her helplessness, her just-below-the-surface bubbling anger or her genuine and horrible suffering. I also didn't want to have the impact that she had on her family, particularly on my mother. I did not want my daughter to take on the yoke of responsibility and resent me for it. I had already watched three generational scenarios: My great-grandmother's influence on my grandmother, both of their influences on my mother and all three of their influences on me. The one that scared me most was the next one—the weight of all four of us on my 11-year-old daughter.

In addition to support, the therapy focused on developing an understanding of the commonalities I shared with each woman, appreciating aspects of our shared legacies as some of the things I most valued in myself. I also had to articulate the differences between myself and each of them. I worked to understand that depression did not negate me, it just made my life different and difficult—hopefully, for a limited amount of time, and that no one genetically, biologically or psychologically is the blueprint for anyone else. Being haunted is not the same as being cursed.

The fact that in little more than a year's time, I descended into a very serious depression does not negate the impact of the psychotherapy or the medicine. For reasons that were never clear, I began to metabolize my medications so rapidly that to keep a therapeutic dose in my blood, I required doses that became untenable. The benefits of each new medicine bottomed out within a matter of weeks

My daughter tried to tease me, tempt me, annoy me, entertain me and soothe me—all to no avail. Her constant question was, "Why are you so sad?" No wonder that I worried about the impact of my depression on her. The self-absorption caused by the acute pain of a severe depression makes being a good parent very difficult. I had difficulty following the rambling conversations in the car that I usually loved. Her new friends' names were hard to remember. Our 11-year-old bedtime ritual, with its whispers, soft songs and backrubs dwindled down to a quick goodnight.

She and my husband hovered and worried. In reaction to my early experience of whispered adult conversations, my husband and I tried to be straightforward with Keara. I remembered what my mother had wished for in her adolescence—"Just some knowledge. What's going on and what's being done to help it."

Now, five years since my last serious depression, my daughter teases us that we went a bit overboard in providing the information my mother had wanted. She insists that the information we gave her about depression was a lot like the information we gave her about sex—a lot of big words with little context. Her concerns had less to do with having a technical command of depression than about the continuity of her care and protection. At the age of 16, she spoke to an interviewer who was writing a story about my depression: "The thing about having someone close to you suffer from depression is that your feelings go from worried, to angrily impatient, to guilty. One of the worst things was seeing my mom in so much pain and being constantly reminded that it wasn't my fault and there was nothing I could do to make her feel better."

We tried to keep her life as stable as possible. Given my mother's experience, I definitely did not want my daughter to "rise to the occasion." In the interview, Keara said: "My mom worked hard to take care of me, to make sure I was taken care of, which I was. I was so lucky to have my father. My parents always shunned the value system where the mother would be the singular child raiser. I was always close to my dad, even closer at the time because I spent more time with him as my mom got worse. Anyway, the shift in my standard of living was not too dramatic."

Sinking into Illness

Despite pills, therapy, love, professional expertise and faith, my symptoms worsened. I didn't sleep more than two hours a night. I stopped eating—it was too hard to swallow. I thought about the wisecrack about someone who is "out of it": the lights are on, but nobody's home. In depression, the lights are off, but somebody's definitely home. She just can't make it to the door to let you in.

My ruminations turned to comforting thoughts of death. I had always thought of myself as living in a series of concentric circles that connected me to life. My outermost circles included my interests and acquaintances, my work and goals. Then came my friends. Then my parents and siblings. Then my husband and daughter. As the depression worsened, those connections dissolved. They were no longer reasons to stay in the game. Life could go on without me.

In the final days before my hospitalization, I was staying alive for my husband and my daughter. I never told them this. In the last days, I kept going only for my daughter. My daughter and her songs. Every morning, Keara stumbles semi-conscious into the bathroom and turns on the shower. Within the space of 30 seconds, she starts to sing. She starts out humming so softly that her voice blends with the spray as it bounces off the wall. And then she chooses her song—sometimes sweet and lyrical, sometimes loud and rocking. Each morning, when I had to face another day on two hours of sleep and no hope, I leaned against the bathroom door waiting for her to sing and let her voice invite me to try for one more day.

The Solution

One morning, finally convinced that suicide was an act of love, not hate, I leaned for what I thought would be the last time against the door. I tried to memorize that voice, with all of its exuberance and hope. And then I realized that ending my life would silence that voice, perhaps forever. And I knew what I had to do. I would finally agree to electroconvulsive therapy (ECT), which had been recommended to me for several weeks. I had always said I'd step in front of a moving train for the sake of my child. Now it was time to prove it.

ECT was the tractor that pulled me out of the mud. Its power was hard to believe. Within several treatments, I was adding 20 to 30 minutes to my sleep per night. Having lost 30 pounds in three months, I began to look forward to meals. My face, which felt like a mask, regained its elasticity. It was as if several heavy backpacks had been taken from my shoulders. But it wasn't a magic cure. I still had to walk the whole way home—a journey that took more than a year, assisted greatly by medicine, therapy and the support of many people.

Readjusting to Family Life

Finding my place again in my family took some time. When her bedtime approached on my first night home from the hospital, Keara announced, "I don't need you to tuck me into bed anymore. I do it myself now." For several weeks, no one raised a voice or broke a rule. I was being watched very carefully. At some point, my daughter must have experienced a critical mass of the old me. She started challenging me again, testing the limits of my authority and my capacity for following through.

Over the course of that year, I had to struggle with self-recriminations about the ways I had failed the people I loved. I was ashamed that I'd been unavailable to Keara and embarrassed that she had seen me so vulnerable. As a psychologist whose profession has historically enjoyed the sport of mother-bashing, it was easy to revert to it myself. Keara would be ruined for life and it would be all my fault.

For a long time after my hospitalization, my daughter dropped her middle name, Manning, and began making it clear that her name came only from my husband, Keara *Depenbrock*. I knew how important it was for her to see herself as separate from me currently—but more important, in the future. It was helpful for my husband to point out to me that although some of it was due to my depression, it was also a normal function of adolescence. When she wrote, "While I have a lot in common with my mother, I have inherited my father's mental health," I was able to see it as a fact as well as a wish.

Over the next several years, I marveled at my child's blooming, despite the scarcity of light in our house at a critical point in her development. Keara later remembered: "My mom's depression was definitely an impediment to us being close at the time. Because she wasn't available to me, and because something so horrible was happening inside of her, it was really hard for her to have this great relationship with other people. I think that she spent all the time and energy she had with me and for me—but it wasn't as much as I wanted. I don't blame her for that. She didn't make a choice to be that way. But sometimes I'd get really frustrated and impatient with her anyway."

I recalled psychoanalyst D.W. Winnicott, one of the less judgmental voices in the psychological wilderness, who disputed the necessity of a perfect mother for a child's healthy development, substituting the more attainable standard of "good-enough mother." My faith in Winnicott was confirmed the night my daughter invited me back into her room for the nightly ritual that had taken so much effort only months before. Now, smoothing her rumpled sheets, straightening her comforter to her exact specifications and rubbing her back with the precise level of finger pressure were gifts, not burdens.

The War Is Never Won

Depression and I are not finished with each other. In 1993, two years after my first round of ECT, I started sliding in the same dangerous direction. This time, we all saw it coming. If I didn't improve quickly, we knew the plan. This time, I had more ECT treatments, on an outpatient basis. I left for the hospital in the morning, after I'd seen Keara off to school, and I was back before she returned home. Life was not business as usual, but we managed the details with the help of our families and friends.

With the addition of a mood stabilizer (lithium), which I had refused after my first ECT, I have since enjoyed the best years of my life. They have also been the best years of my relationship with my daughter. There was something in the combination of vulnerability and stability that protected us. She saw me go to hell. But she was there for the return trip as well. Her fears of depression invading our family again were confirmed so quickly that in some ironic way she got to really learn the drill and find comfort in the evidence that our plans worked. We both learned that lousy things can happen and that they can be so bad and so powerful that they stand good solid relationships on their heads.

The differences between Keara and me are clear. Temperamentally, she resembles my husband and my mother, not me. That knowledge frees her from having to deny the ways in which we are so alike. She can claim our similarities without the fear of turning into me. At the end of her senior year, she came home, leaned against the kitchen counter while I peeled carrots and described having to fill out a form with her name exactly as she wanted it on her high school diploma. "I was afraid it wouldn't all fit," she told me.

"Yeah, Keara Depenbrock is a mouthful," I replied.

"No, Mom," she laughed, "it's worse than that. My *real* name, Keara *Manning* Depenbrock."

Our children inhale our imperfections and failings as easily as our love. Perhaps they are meant to. How else will they ever learn to tolerate themselves? My goal is no longer to make a perfect impression. Now, I'm shooting for an imperfect impression and helping my daughter deal with it. I look ahead and hope that she is spared the torment of severe depression. I think she will be. But on the chance that she might get lost in it, or in any of the other ways life tests our faith and our patience and our endurance, I wish for her exactly what she gave to me: a sweet voice in the distance that penetrates her darkness and calls her gently toward home.

A Psychologist's Turn to Talk

Kay Redfield Jamison

Kay Redfield Jamison, a professor of psychiatry at Johns Hopkins University School of Medicine in Baltimore, Maryland, is the author of *An Unquiet Mind: A Memoir of Moods and Madness*. In the following selection, she explains that for a long time, her visible position as a professor and psychiatrist prevented her from revealing her history of manic-depression. Eventually, however, Jamison decided to go public, telling her personal story in the *Washington Post*. Although she was afraid of the reaction from colleagues, patients, and the public, she writes that the overall response was positive. Furthermore, she asserts, the act of speaking out about her own illness gave her a sense of freedom that she had not felt before.

As a practicing clinical psychologist, I was extremely reluctant to go public about having a severe, psychotic form of manic-depressive illness, a genetic condition characterized by dramatic swings in mood, energy and behavior. That it would be difficult to tell people, I assumed. That it would be less difficult than continuing to remain silent, I hoped.

At 48, I had studied and written about depression and manic-depression for 20 years, was a full professor with clinical privileges at a university teaching hospital and had the unequivocal support of my husband, family, friends and department chairman. My illness had been under good control for many years. If I couldn't go public about it now, how could others hope to do so?

I decided, finally, to write a book about it. I also agreed to talk with a *Washington Post* journalist who was doing a story about my work. I hoped that by revealing my own experiences, I could let others know what having such a devastating yet intriguing illness was like.

Revealing the Truth

To say the least, the disorder had brought a certain level of emotional intensity into my life. It had also brought psychotic manias and suicidal depressions. From the time I was 16, my life had been an unpre-

Reprinted from Kay Redfield Jamison, "A Psychologist's Turn to Talk," *American Health*, January/February 1997, by permission.

dictable, often terrifying, occasionally glorious storm of moods, thoughts and behaviors. Yet despite this, thanks to excellent psychiatric care and highly effective medication, I'd managed to keep my illness hidden, except from a few friends and the physicians I worked with closely. The thought of now telling my colleagues and patients filled me with horror. I knew that once I'd told them the truth, their perceptions of me would never be the same again.

I should have realized that the various responses would be complicated: uncomfortably silent, funny, insensitive, generous, wonderful, cruel. They would, in short, be very human. A few days after the *Post* story appeared, for instance, my gardener approached me outside my house. Referring both to the article and to my rather manic tendency in the late summer months to order, with great enthusiasm, hundreds of vivid spring bulbs, he said, "Gosh, Dr. Jamison. If I'd known that you had *that* kind of problem, I would have planted more subdued colors." It was a perfect comment, perfectly unexpected, and one that still makes me laugh whenever I think about it.

Telling my patients turned out to be not nearly as difficult as I imagined. Most of them were stunned. "You seem so normal," said one. "So Brooks Brothers-ish." Two patients, fellow professors, expressed the hope that the academic community would become more aware of the extent of mental illness within its ranks. Most asked me what medication I was on (lithium) and wondered what side effects I'd experienced. But I was amazed, in every instance, how quickly our psychotherapy sessions reverted to their usual form and focus. My patients were eager to get on with the business of their lives.

Still, I dreaded going back to work once the *Post* article came out. That first day, I found myself slinking along the corridors of the hospital, identification badge flipped over so my name was hidden, trying to be inconspicuous. When I walked into the psychiatric residents' seminar that I teach with a colleague, there was silence, and I could feel the discomfort in the room. Soon, however, I lost myself in the topic at hand—the cardiac complications of antidepressants, with its numbing discussion of plasma levels and arrhythmias—and that initial unease was replaced with warmth and an unspoken support. The teaching rounds later that afternoon were likewise distracting and reassuringly collegial. My self-consciousness began to fade, replaced by the more usual sense of delight I find in teaching.

For the most part, it became easier still. The following week, the chief resident dropped by my office to congratulate me. It should not have had to be a brave thing to do, she said, but it probably was. She told me she had distributed the *Post* article to all of the residents, several of whom suffered from mood disorders themselves. A few days later, I had a long discussion with another resident, who confessed that he had struggled with severe depression for years. For the first time, I clearly saw the good that might come from my disclosure.

Widespread Understanding

Several weeks later, I went to the annual meeting of the American Psychiatric Association in Miami. I knew that news travels fast, and I was not eager to face people. Yet those colleagues who actually approached me were supportive. Most said they'd had absolutely no idea that I had manic-depressive illness, and most thought my decision to be open about it was a good one. Many spontaneously hugged me and wished me well. A few, however, seemed suddenly uncomfortable, averting their eyes and saying nothing. I found the silence chilling; it remains an ongoing, if increasingly less frequent, source of pain to me.

Then there was the sheer number of people who called to request clinical consultations—more than 50 in the first five days after the *Post* article. I heard from doctors, attorneys, students, scientists, teachers and businessmen, almost all of whom described fears about repercussions in their work life if colleagues found out they suffered from mental illness. Some worried about being asked to leave medical school, others that their professional licenses would be taken away. Many others—including several members of Congress—simply called or wrote to offer their support.

The response was even more dramatic with the publication of my memoir, *An Unquiet Mind: A Memoir of Moods and Madness*, in October of 1995. Within weeks, letters flooded in—nearly 3,000 as of 1996. Most of the writers shared their own or family members' experiences with depression and manic-depression; the level of despair and frustration was palpable. Hundreds sent manuscripts, poems or artwork that they had composed while manic, depressed or recovering from their illness. Some letters, however, were vicious, saying that because manic-depression was a genetic illness, it was a "blessing that I hadn't had children," that I'd "spared the world of yet another destructive psychotic." Their cruelty hurt, and I occasionally found myself shaking or crying after reading a particularly vitriolic response.

The Freedom of Opening Up

But all things considered, speaking out about my illness has had a freeing effect. I'm much more able to say what I feel now. And for every discomfort about the loss of privacy, for every fear of a personal or professional reprisal, there is also relief in the honesty. For the most part, people have been more understanding than I could have imagined.

The process has also drawn my family more tightly together. We've begun talking about an illness that for far too long we ignored or skirted around. It's become a part of our casual conversation, a more natural part of our lives. A few months after my "coming out," for instance, my 11-year-old niece wrote a school report about manic-depressive illness, expressing herself with a frankness and knowledge unimaginable to me at that age. "This report," she wrote, "tells the stories of my family's pains and triumphs. It tells of the sorrows caused by manic-depressive illness, which has sometimes torn my family apart. But this report also explains that even in the face of this fatal disease, people can succeed."

My niece has already succeeded not only in being honest about her family, but also in making me very glad that I have finally been more honest about myself.

CHAPTER 3

TREATMENTS FOR DEPRESSION

THE FIRST STEPS TOWARD THERAPY AND WELLNESS

Michael D. Yapko

Depression is an illness that requires professional help, according to clinical psychologist Michael Yapko. Symptoms such as suicidal thoughts and drastic changes in sleeping and eating patterns, he writes, indicate that treatment is necessary. Yapko emphasizes that while there are various approaches to treatment, including the use of antidepressant medication, the first step is to find a suitable therapist to guide the patient through the process of getting help. Yapko writes for various psychology journals and is widely known for his work on treating depression with active, brief therapy.

How do you know when to get professional help? As a general answer, *you should seek help long before things get really bad.* To be more specific, there are at least five factors to consider when you are deciding whether you should seek professional treatment.

The Five Factors

Suicidal Thoughts or Feelings. If you often find yourself thinking about death, killing yourself, or fantasizing about the relief of being dead and not having to deal with your emotional distress anymore, then you are experiencing suicidal thoughts. They should not preoccupy you, so if you have them often, they are a legitimate basis for concern. If they are vivid thoughts, detailed to the point where you have even thought of specific ways to kill yourself and the consequences of your death, then such suicidal thoughts are an even greater reason for immediate concern. It would be wise for you to give them immediate attention in therapy.

Suicide has appropriately been called "the permanent solution to a temporary problem." To believe hopelessly that your future holds only more pain is distorted, depressed thinking. Suicide is a global, irreversible, and terrible solution to specific problems. If you are at all suicidal, I urge you to get into therapy *immediately,* where your self-destructive thoughts and feelings can be addressed and resolved as quickly as possible. *Think preventively.*

Acute Depression Turning Chronic. If your depression had a rapid onset following a traumatic event (such as the death of a loved one, the breakup of an important relationship, the loss of a job, an illness or accident, or *any* other such personally distressing event), then your depression, though painful in the short run, could be considered a normal response to painful circumstances. However, if you interpret your feelings incorrectly, and the depression continues beyond a reasonable length of time—from a few weeks to a few months—then there is concern that an acute (short-term) situation may be becoming a chronic (long-term) one.

Most people who suffer a depressive episode experience a full return to their normal level of functioning in a few weeks or months at most. Some individuals, however, never seem to "bounce back" completely. If you feel that your experience of depression is lasting longer than it should, or if you worry that it will, it may be wise to get a professional opinion. Or if you recognize you are making lifelong negative decisions or pronouncements during a depression ("I'll never be happy again"), then it's important to get help from someone who can challenge you to think more clearly.

Lifestyle Disruption. If your experience of depression is severe enough to impair your ability to function well in various areas of your life, it would be best to *seek help well before life situations deteriorate further.* Losing your marriage, losing your job, or abusing your body and physical health with drugs or apathy because of depression will only add to your problems. Take steps *now* to prevent the downward spiral, which could cause you more hurt and pain than the depression already has.

Reality Testing. If you are in a position of relative isolation and there isn't anyone close enough for you to talk with about your thoughts and feelings, then you have no one with whom you can "reality test." Reality testing means checking out your perceptions with others who have a more objective viewpoint. . . . Speaking to someone with an objective view can be extremely valuable in getting you back on track. A good therapist can be a valuable partner for reality testing, particularly if he is experienced in recognizing the common distortions in depressed people's thinking.

Because it may be beyond the range of your capabilities at this time to step outside your own (depressing) frame of reference, seek someone to help you effectively. A person outside your frame of reference can provide feedback that is refreshingly beyond anything you are able to generate on your own. A fresh pair of eyes on your problems can allow for fresh solutions. Furthermore, a caring relationship, like the collaborative partnership of good therapy, has healing qualities that go far beyond what you can experience on your own. (And if relationship problems are a primary source of distress in your life, how do you solve relationship problems *by yourself?*)

Extreme Symptoms. Many of the symptoms associated with depression can exist on a physiological level. If you are severely depressed—unable to sleep well, without appetite, with no energy, unable to concentrate, or feeling just plain lousy—then you may benefit from more immediate interventions of a biological type, such as antidepressant medications. They may help you achieve a more receptive state to the additional benefits of psychotherapy, which I would encourage you to pursue simultaneously.

Once you make the decision to seek professional treatment, you will need a strategy to help you find competent help. The information in the next section will be helpful.

Approaches to Treatment

It is little wonder that people are confused by the intricacies of the mental health field. After all, there are many categories of mental health professionals, each with a different title and educational background, and each with different ways of looking at problems like depression. There are psychiatrists, psychologists, marriage and family therapists, pastoral counselors, lay counselors, and social workers. All are called "psychotherapists," defined as those who provide therapeutic intervention for emotional disorders or psychological problems.

How can you know which is the best psychotherapist for you? In a broad generalization, we can divide the mental health field into two major areas, biological and psychological. The areas have a great deal of overlap, but I exaggerate their differences here in order to clarify some points. Bear in mind that they are not mutually exclusive approaches, nor should they be. Biological, psychological, and sociological factors all contribute to depression.

Biological Approaches to Treatment

The primary psychotherapeutic practitioner in the biological realm is the psychiatrist, a person with an M.D. A physician who specializes in the diagnosis and treatment of psychological disturbances, according to a medical model, the psychiatrist has had advanced training in the use of psychoactive medications (drugs that affect the mind) and physically based treatments for psychological disturbances. Psychiatrists also learn psychotherapy techniques to complement their use of medications.

In the case of depression, the psychiatrist's primary tool is antidepressant medication. In cases of severe and unrelenting depression (where the person is unable to function), the treatment may also be severe, calling for hospitalization and even, in extreme cases, the use of electroconvulsive treatment (ECT), commonly known as "shock treatment." While ECT has historically been the subject of fear and horror stories, many clinicians and researchers have come to believe that ECT is the "treatment of choice" in very severe depressions. It remains a controversial treatment, though, and is usually advised only in the most extreme cases. *Only* a psychiatrist can administer ECT.

For the great majority of severely depressed individuals, the condition is managed by psychiatrists with the use of antidepressant medications, which have repeatedly been shown, in the best of clinical studies, to be effective in providing relief from the symptoms of depression. While it is not yet fully understood how such medications work, most depressed individuals can experience relatively rapid relief (in two to six weeks) with their use. Thus, if your depression is highly disruptive to your life and you are experiencing uncomfortable symptoms, particularly on a physiological level, you may consider consulting a psychiatrist for an evaluation as to the appropriate use of antidepressant medication. . . .

Medications Involve Risks

There are a number of concerns to be aware of in using medications. While antidepressant medications may provide marked symptom relief in a relatively short period of time, they do not significantly change your attributional style, cognitive style, relationship style, and other key patterns. Despite the media hype for drugs like Prozac, which can be effective for many people, the potential for a recurrence of depression is higher if you receive only antidepressant medications and no additional psychotherapy.

Another concern is that the medications have side effects that, until you adjust to them, may be a source of discomfort. The newer antidepressants, such as the selective serotonin reuptake inhibitors (SSRIs, like Prozac and Zoloft), have fewer side effects than the older tricyclic antidepressants (TCAs). Fewer side effects means a higher likelihood of your being able to continue on the drug, which increases its chances of working. For most people, the issue of side effects is a minor consideration.

A final point about medications: I am concerned that the medication may discourage the client from actively striving to change his depression-causing patterns. The use of medications alone may encourage you to assume a passive role in treatment at a time when it is critical that you actively learn new and healthy life-management skills. I emphasize *action!*

There are other forms of physical intervention beyond drugs and ECT, such as physical exercise, diet, and changes in sleep schedules. I acknowledge these as potentially useful in a general way, so I encourage you to be active in pursuing exercise, rest, and a good diet regimen.

Psychological Approaches to Treatment

Psychological approaches to treatment assume that your emotional disturbance is a product of your experience, including the things you learned as well as the things you did not learn from life. These approaches primarily involve "talk therapy," usually an exchange between therapist and client of ideas, perspectives, and philosophies. . . .

There are dozens of types of psychological therapies, each with its own assumptions and approaches. Since the typical depressed individual does not know the differences between approaches, he may be confused about what the "best" therapy is. . . . Not all therapies are equally effective, and some *are* better than others for depression.

If you imagine therapy to be a matter of your confessing all your problems and going on endlessly about what your parents did to you when you were growing up, then your idea about therapy is common but inaccurate. Of the many different approaches to treatment, the ones that work best for depression do not rely on such past-oriented methods. They involve building a future that is compelling and positive.

In pointing out that there are many different types of therapy, I want to suggest that the type of therapy you seek for depression is important to your eventual recovery. More important than the type itself, though, is the nature and level of skill of the therapist with whom you work. Cognitive, behavioral, and interpersonal models of psychotherapy have *consistently* been shown to be the most effective in treating depression. There are many qualified professionals trained in these approaches, including all levels and backgrounds of psychotherapists (psychologists, psychiatrists, family therapists, and social workers). The academic degree of the person you consult (Ph.D., M.D., M.A., L.C.S.W.) may be of importance to you *if* you equate level of education with level of expertise. It is *not* a reliable indicator, however. There are some highly educated but unskilled clinicians, and there are some lesser educated but highly skilled clinicians. It is more important that the therapist be able to apply efficiently the principles and methods of these therapies; a more advanced or specialized degree does *not* offer assurance that this will be the case. I directly suggest to you that it is less the academic degree and more the professional skills of the individual that will determine how effectively he conducts the therapy.

Shopping for a Therapist

It is unfortunate that at a time when you are probably least motivated and energized, you most need to expend energy in "shopping" for a therapist. Finding a good therapist is not always an easy task. There are many questions to ask, many factors to take into account, and many possibilities to consider. Therapy can and should be done actively *and* briefly in most cases. Spending time going over endless details about your unhappy past is unnecessary, unless you need to explore it or vent your feelings about it. Focusing on hurt, anger, or any other negative feeling can amplify it and still not teach you any new skills or correct any distortions. Therefore, it is reasonable to ask for specific information from potential therapists about how they would approach the treatment of your depression.

A good place to start your search is a referral. Your family physician may have psychotherapists to whom he refers patients. Physicians, who often have an exclusively medical or biological viewpoint, are more likely to recommend a psychiatrist and the use of antidepressant medication. That's fine, but you'll still need a therapist to talk to if the psychiatrist you see doesn't also employ psychotherapy. You may raise the subject with friends or relatives you trust who themselves have had experience with therapy. Perhaps you're new to your area and don't know anyone you can ask for a referral. In that case, I recommend that you call some professional organizations and groups and seek a referral from one of them.

Preliminary Research

If you use the phonebook as a reference source, you can look up "Psychologists," "Counselors," "Mental Health," and related headings, and then call specific psychotherapists, especially if they advertise themselves as interpersonal, cognitive, or behavioral therapists. When you call, you can ask for certain basic information, such as the therapist's academic degree, (even though *which* advanced degree one has doesn't matter so much, an advanced degree *is* important), whether he has been licensed by the state to do psychotherapy, and what his treatment of depressed clients usually involves. (See *only* a state-licensed, reputable clinician.) It is unrealistic to expect that a therapist will spend an inordinate amount of time with you on the telephone, but it is not at all unreasonable to ask for just a few minutes of the therapist's time to get some basic information and a sample of his professional demeanor.

You can ask the average length of treatment, the fee per session, whether any health insurance you have will cover the costs (and, if so, what your cost share might be), how your progress in therapy will be evaluated, the frequency of sessions, and the general availability of the therapist for regular appointments.

Once you have this sort of information, you can tell whether to schedule a first appointment. During that appointment, you can expect to describe your experience of depression, including your symptoms, your ideas of what your depression is about, the things you have already done to try to get over it, and so forth. During this first session, you should also get an idea, from the way the therapist responds, whether he will be able to provide you with support, feedback, direction, structured learning activities, and other key ingredients of successful therapy.

It may not be easy, but keep in mind that while you are intelligently evaluating whether you can work effectively with a therapist, many of the cognitive distortions and negative relationship patterns that may be a part of your depression can creep into the therapeutic relationship. It is important, therefore, that you maintain an awareness of your need to set limits, avoid emotional reasoning, keep from jumping to conclusions, and do no personalizing on the basis of feedback you get from your therapist.

If you find that your response to this person, based on his treatment of you, is negative, or if you feel that his level of expertise is not enough to meet your needs, then it is not only desirable but *necessary* for you to interview more therapists. Do not allow yourself to be manipulated by a therapist speaking "psychobabble" who attempts to convince you that it is your depression that prevents you from forming a meaningful therapy relationship with him. It is very important to your therapy's success that you feel valued, supported, and positively challenged to grow by your therapist. You must definitely have the feeling your therapist is on your side, especially when you're dealing with tough issues.

A therapeutic relationship is a special type of relationship, but it follows many of the principles of other positive and healthy relationships. A good therapist is, in most ways, an educator, *not* a substitute parent. It is important to have within the therapy relationship the same expectations of acceptance and respect that you want in any relationship. That's why it's imperative that you be clear about setting limits. You are half of the therapy relationship, so even though the therapist has greater expertise in an area of vital interest to you—namely, depression—that is *not* a legitimate basis for him to discount or ignore your needs or views. After all, you know your experience, background, and thoughts better than anyone else ever will. You are the expert on you. It is your job to educate the therapist about who you are and how you do things so that he can get a good sense of where and how to intervene. If the therapist repeatedly goes off on things you find irrelevant or unnecessarily hurtful, you can say so. Be an *active* participant in your therapy.

The therapy relationship is a confidential one; whatever you say about yourself *must*, both by law and professional code, be kept in the strictest confidence. There are only two exceptions in which confidence may be broken: if you threaten harm either to yourself or to someone else; and if you are abusing a child or an elderly person. Thus, for all intents and purposes, nothing that you talk about will ever go beyond the therapist. When he provides you with a secure environment in which to explore distorted perceptions, depressing beliefs, and self-limiting patterns, and when he teaches effective life-management skills, remember that the likelihood of your recovery is great.

Therapy Depends on the Patient

It is worth remembering, too, that the therapy relationship is based on your problems and needs. You can take an active role in shaping the direction of the treatment, even though you may not know what things you need to learn or how to best learn them. Therapy is not something that is done *to* you. It is a process in which you participate. Your input, your willingness to self-disclose, and your eagerness to carry out well-intentioned therapeutic assignments are all vital to the process. It is one of the great paradoxes in the world of therapy that even the best of therapists can help only to the extent the client permits.

It bears repeating that therapies are as subjective as the therapists who practice them. No psychiatrist can predict exactly how you will respond to a particular medication, and no psychologist can predict exactly how long it will take you to learn a new skill. If you try something and it does not work, do something else. If you go for therapy, give it a reasonable chance to succeed. You should expect to see some positive results in six to twelve weeks of treatment. If the experience does not prove to be beneficial, do not overgeneralize, in a distorted way, that it is a negative statement about the value of *all* therapy. Nor should you personalize, in a distorted way, that therapy works for everyone else but that somehow you cannot benefit from it.

You now have many explicit criteria to help you be a smart consumer of therapy services. There are lots of very skilled, very talented therapists out there. With a little bit of persistence and some self-awareness of your needs and, therefore, the kinds of approaches you might best respond to, you will, I have no doubt, find the quality help that you want.

VARIETIES OF TALK THERAPY

John H. Greist and James W. Jefferson

In the following selection, excerpted from their book *Depression and Its Treatment*, John Greist and James Jefferson provide a breakdown of the basic categories of psychotherapy. They write that psychotherapy, also known as "talk" therapy, usually takes one of five approaches: supportive, dynamic, interpersonal, cognitive-behavioral, or behavior therapy. With all the attention given to antidepressants in recent years, the authors state, psychotherapy seems to have taken a back seat in the treatment of depression. However, Greist and Jefferson maintain, talk therapy and medication should not be thought of as competing against each other; rather, the two can be combined for effective treatment. Greist and Jefferson, both professors of psychiatry at the University of Wisconsin Medical School in Madison, codirect the Lithium Center and the Obsessive-Compulsive Center.

Psychotherapy is sometimes referred to as "talk" therapy. Patients and their doctors talk about the experiences patients have had and are having, important relationships, and future goals, as well as the feelings, thoughts, and behaviors they produce. Psychotherapies are usually most helpful for less severe depressions, which form the largest part of the depressive spectrum. Psychotherapies alone are less effective for more severe depressions, but may be helpful in improving relationships, thinking patterns, or behaviors that may have led to depression. General support of depressed patients is always beneficial and may sustain them through their suffering even if other treatments are ineffective. Education about depression and its treatment is an important part of all psychotherapies.

Although psychotherapies are frequently provided to depressed patients, and many clinicians believe in their usefulness, there have been fewer scientific studies of their effectiveness compared with the studies of the effectiveness of antidepressant medications and electroconvulsive therapy. There are scores of specific named psychotherapies. However, most psychotherapies are variations on one of the following five approaches.

Supportive Psychotherapy. All patients need and deserve support and empathic understanding while they are depressed. Supportive psychotherapy helps by shoring up defenses, utilizing strengths, empathizing with distress, explaining the course of depression, monitoring changes, and reassuring the patient that improvement will, in time, occur. It also helps the doctor learn the effects of other treatments from the patient. With the patient's permission, support and explanation should also be provided to family members, friends, and others important in the patient's life. These individuals constitute a network of support more available than anything the doctor can provide. When other treatments are ineffective, support by caring others can sustain a person until depression resolves on its own with the passage of time. All doctors provide support to their patients. Family doctors often know patients best and are, therefore, a most important source of support.

Dynamic Psychotherapy. Dynamic therapies seek to understand unresolved unconscious conflicts that may lead to depression. Depression is often described as anger turned inward, and it is felt that helping the individual uncover, understand, and deal more appropriately with angry feelings may lead to recovery from depression. Interpretation of dreams, free association, and exploration of the past are important techniques of psychoanalytic psychotherapy. Other psychodynamic psychotherapists may use the same techniques but focus more on present relationships and role functioning. Patients are helped to understand the possible role of these factors in their depression and to find new ways of dealing with people and feelings. Dynamic psychotherapy may continue for periods ranging from a few months to several years.

Short-Term Therapies

By definition, short-term therapies are limited in length. They often last from a few weeks to several months (commonly 10 to 20 sessions), focus more on the present rather than the past, and usually involve an active collaboration between patient and therapist. Patients are encouraged to put forward their view of the problems they face and the therapist explores alternative explanations in a warm, interested, and respectful manner. Other common characteristics of short-term therapies include defining concrete and measurable targets for treatment, setting modest and achievable goals before progressing to more difficult problems, identifying and correcting obvious deficiencies such as poor anger control and lack of assertiveness, and regularly providing feedback regarding problems and progress in therapy. Three short-term therapies have shown effectiveness in careful research studies.

Interpersonal Psychotherapy. This approach uses both supportive and dynamic psychotherapeutic techniques. Because depression occurs in the context of relationships (poor relationships may lead to depression and depression may damage relationships), emphasis is placed on understanding and improving the relationship skills of the patient. Goals are to reduce depressive symptoms, improve self-esteem, and help the patient develop new strategies for improving social and interpersonal functioning. Individuals with ingrained and severe personality problems would usually not be treated with interpersonal psychotherapy. Specific techniques are available to help with problems of grief, role changes, interpersonal disputes, and deficits the patient may have in interpersonal functioning. Both short- and long-term scientific studies have found beneficial effects from the use of interpersonal psychotherapy to treat depression. There is some evidence that combining interpersonal psychotherapy with antidepressant medication offers further advantages.

Cognitive-Behavioral Therapy. Cognitive-behavioral therapists help patients by focusing on their negative "cognitions" or thoughts about themselves, the world, and the future. Negative thoughts about oneself lead to lowered self-esteem; depressed people often feel defective and lacking in positive attributes that they believe everyone else has in abundance. Negative thoughts about the world lead to excessive caution and guardedness; those who are depressed view the glass as "half empty" and describe life as demanding and depriving. Typically, they place a negative interpretation on ambiguous events that others would view more neutrally or even positively. Negative thoughts about the future lead to pessimism and hopelessness; when depressed, many are convinced that the feelings they have will continue forever and that they deserve this fate. Cognitive therapists believe that these negative thoughts can precipitate and perpetuate depression.

To understand the cognitive perspective on depression, you might conduct an exercise of immersing yourself in consistently negative cognitions for 5 minutes to determine what effect this process has on your mood. Most people find the experience somewhat depressing and can understand how a preoccupation with such pessimistic themes can contribute to depression. Specific educational, cognitive, and behavioral techniques have been combined to counteract the negative thoughts so common in depression and the behaviors that result from negative thinking. Usually, behaviors are changed first before focused work begins on cognitions or thoughts, which, in turn, precedes improvements in mood. For example, an individual who reports "I can't do anything," when asked to be more specific might offer, "I used to love to cook but now I have no interest in cooking and couldn't even take the first step if I did. I feel useless and know I'll never feel better." The cognitive-behavioral therapist would seek this patient's agreement to initiate a graded task assignment requiring a tiny behavior such as "boiling water." This behavioral step must be taken without sarcasm and with empathy for the distress the patient is experiencing, and the difficulty such a seemingly simple task may represent for this patient. A number of scientific studies have shown a beneficial effect of cognitive therapy in treating mild to moderately severe depression. Cognitive therapy does not appear to be effective for severe depression.

Comparing the Effectiveness of Treatments

The National Institute of Mental Health has supported a multicenter study of the effectiveness of well-trained therapists providing interpersonal psychotherapy or cognitive-behavioral therapy or imipramine (a tricyclic antidepressant) or placebo (an inactive substance). Results indicate that both interpersonal psychotherapy and imipramine were effective in the treatment of mild, moderate, and severe depression. However, "severe," as defined in this study, did not include the most severely depressed patients, who were thought so unlikely to respond to psychotherapy that they were excluded.

Cognitive-behavioral therapy produced significant improvement for patients with mild or moderate depression but not those suffering "severe" depression.

Interestingly, even the placebo treatment produced significant improvement although fewer placebo patients recovered fully. The explanation for this finding may lie in the supportive contact the patients received from the doctors who were monitoring their placebo medication. Overall, patients who received either type of psychotherapy or imipramine showed trends toward better outcome at the end of treatment than patients who received placebo. However, the differences between the patients who received treatment and those receiving placebo "were often not statistically significant, especially for the psychotherapies." Also, the benefit from the psychotherapies, especially for cognitive-behavioral therapy, was less consistent than for treatment with imipramine. This means that the matching of patient and psychotherapist has an effect on outcome, which is not as much of an issue when imipramine, a medication, is the main treatment.

Behavior Therapy. Depressed patients have changes in their behaviors, and behavior therapy attempts to alleviate depression by returning behavior patterns toward normal. This approach helps patients increase the number of normal and nondepressed behaviors so that they will receive the positive reinforcements from thoughts and feelings associated with more normal behavior patterns. Behavioral techniques are used to increase enjoyable activities, decrease or minimize the effects of unpleasant events, increase rewards for achieving goals, enhance social skills, use time more effectively and efficiently, and develop cognitive approaches similar to those used in formal cognitive therapy.

Because there are so many components of behavioral therapy of depression, it is difficult to arrive at firm conclusions about the effectiveness of behavior therapy as a whole. Nevertheless, most studies have indicated that behavior therapy of depression is superior to no treatment.

Treatment Is Essential

Whatever else happens in psychotherapy, the patient is provided with a relationship with a doctor who has worked with other depressed patients. Through this relationship the therapist provides information about depression and support to patient and family. Psychotherapists also engender hope by providing an explanation for depression and help in pursuing a particular psychotherapeutic approach to the relief of depression.

Final conclusions about the relative effectiveness of psychotherapy and medications for different kinds of depression await further carefully controlled studies. At present, our understanding of the available research suggests:

1. Mild and moderate depression account for about two-thirds of all depression.

2. Although mild depression often disappears without treatment, it may stop sooner with psychotherapy. Mild depression that is long-lasting or unresponsive to psychotherapy may be helped by medication.

3. Moderate and severe depressions usually require treatment with antidepressant medications, which are commonly given in conjunction with psychotherapy. The combination of interpersonal or cognitive therapy with antidepressant medications may be more effective than either treatment alone for moderate depression. Severe depression is unlikely to respond to psychotherapy and should not be treated solely with psychotherapy. Antidepressant medications and electroconvulsive therapy (supplemented with psychotherapy) are critical to the effective treatment of severe depression.

4. Psychotherapy and medication should not be seen as competitive but, rather, as compatible and complementary. Medications are most effective in relieving symptoms of depression while those psychotherapies that have been shown to be effective *may* help patients change aspects of their thinking and ways of relating that make them more vulnerable to depression.

EXPLORING ALTERNATIVE THERAPIES

Peter Carlin

Antidepressants are frequently used as the primary treatment for depression. According to Peter Carlin, however, many patients are finding longer lasting relief in nonconventional treatments. Procedures targeting the body, such as acupuncture and herbal remedies, seem to be effective for many who do not benefit from medications such as Prozac, explains Carlin. For some, he notes, alternative therapies have provided a way to sustain an ongoing level of strong mental health. Ultimately, says Carlin, a holistic approach to depression takes into account the whole person, not just the illness. Carlin, a senior writer for *People* magazine, has written extensively on health issues.

If her pain had ever become unbearable, she knows exactly how she'd have ended it. "It would have to be a gun," Helen Gibson says. "Poison is just too iffy." It's surprising to hear such gloomy words come from an amiable, clear-eyed woman in a sensible blue blazer. But, as Gibson explains, she had reason to consider such scenarios. The Gibsons had always been a close family. Unfortunately, one of the things they shared was chronic depression. "Let's just say that there is a history of suicide attempts in my immediate family," she says.

They lived in Riverdale, Maryland, a hardworking clan of government office workers. Although they never talked about the shadow that loomed over them, when the week ended the Gibsons liked to get together to paint the darkness. "They didn't know what depression was," Gibson recalls. "They just drank, and became alcoholics." For the most part her relatives were happy drunks. But once in a while, come dusk Sunday when the boozy warmth dissipated, a Gibson might become very unhappy indeed.

Helen's Struggle

Helen wanted to be different, and to a great extent she succeeded. She went to college, as no previous Gibson had done. Setting her professional sights on a career as a "do-gooder, but with a solid income," she worked her way up the administrative ladder in the world of Washington, D.C.'s interest groups. As Gibson, now 50, sits in her

Reprinted from Peter Carlin, "Treat the Body, Heal the Mind," *Health*, January/February 1997, by permission of *Health*, ©1997.

glass-walled office at the Communications Workers of America, surrounded by autographed pictures of Robert Kennedy, Hillary Rodham Clinton, and former Texas governor Ann Richards, it's apparent how far she's come. Trouble is, the Gibson family demon came with her. She began seeing a therapist for chronic depression when she was 20. At that time she occasionally stayed in bed for whole days, unable to muster the strength to climb to her feet. Later, even as she got her life on track and her emotions on steadier ground, her illness would sometimes fog her mind and leave her sluggish and forlorn.

Unlike her relatives, Gibson knew her despair was a recognized disease. She came of age in an era when psychiatrists were tracing depression to misfiring neurotransmitters in the brain and making fantastic advances in their ability to revive the synaptic spark with drugs. In 25 years Gibson was put on at least half a dozen antidepressants, from imipramine, the first wonder drug, to Prozac, the revolutionary happy drug that inspired a media frenzy in the mid-nineties. So why didn't the problem go away? Maybe because, as every psychiatrist knows, miracle drugs don't always lead to miracle cures. Sometimes the inevitable side effects—ranging from a chronically dry mouth to panic attacks—became too much for Gibson to bear. More often a drug's uplifting effects would simply fade, and she'd feel herself sinking back into the gloom.

By age 40, she had only to look in the mirror to see that despondency clung to her. She had chronic, painful indigestion and a bad case of asthma, and she was 35 pounds overweight. A cautious woman with a taste for structure, Gibson had for years felt comfortable with psychiatry's drug-oriented, passive-patient approach. But now her questions about the drugs—and about her life—were mounting. Would she ever find a medicine that would continue working? How might decades of constant use of antidepressants affect her health as she got older? "I was tired of relying on drugs," she explains. "I wanted to see if there was something different I could do for myself."

Eventually that wish led her to the Washington, D.C., office of James S. Gordon, a psychiatrist with a radical new approach. The Harvard-trained Gordon is certainly well acquainted with the biological nuances of depression. But for the past 15 years, as founder of the Center for Mind-Body Medicine, Gordon has helped patients replace their drug prescriptions with a program of alternative therapies. And by now he's convinced that holistic medicine can be as effective against depression as antidepressants. Most people with chronic depression, he believes, don't need drugs to feel good.

Trying Out a Holistic Approach

Gordon's approach couldn't be more controversial within psychiatry, where the ability of antidepressant medicine to correct abnormal brain chemistry isn't questioned and the idea of encouraging seriously depressed people to gamble on unproven alternatives is viewed with alarm. Gordon, however, comes at the debate from a different perspective. In his view, misfiring neurotransmitters are not the cause of depression but instead a *symptom* of entire lives that have become unbalanced through ill health, quirky genes, and psychic distress. By that logic, then, a chronically depressed person's best chance at a life-long cure is to marshal every health-enhancing tool on God's green earth—nutritious food, exercise, meditation, acupuncture, human connection—to right her body and brain chemistry, rather than relying on drugs.

"Put someone on medication," Gordon says, "and you're saying, 'Yes, you're depressed. That's who you are, and you need drugs to be normal.' I say the basis of their healing comes from things they can do for themselves."

The first thing Helen Gibson noticed in Jim Gordon's office was a soft table, the type you'd climb on for a massage. None of the psychiatrists she'd consulted had been the least bit touchy-feely, but Gordon, a tall man with soft, boyish features and a wide forehead, believes in the power of touch. Indeed, he's willing to look almost anywhere for useful glimmers of wisdom about people and what helps them mend. On his office bookshelves two decades' worth of the *New England Journal of Medicine* is lined up next to Deepak Chopra's *Quantum Healing*, the *Physician's Desk Reference* leans up against *A Modern Herbal*, Vols. I–II, and several biographies of Sigmund Freud vie for space with a glass statuette of an angel, a wizard, and a chubby Buddha.

Gordon held only a passing interest in alternative medicine until one day in the early seventies when he injured his lower back. For two months he was bent over in extreme pain, and his case stumped even the chief of orthopedics at the local teaching hospital. But when he followed Chinese medicine's prescription for a weeklong all-pineapple diet followed by a visit to an osteopath, and his symptoms eased, he began searching for answers beyond the boundaries of conventional medicine. Now Gordon teaches in a program of mind-body studies at Georgetown University School of Medicine and serves as the chair for an advisory council of the National Institutes of Health's Office of Alternative Medicine. In 1996 he published his tenth book, *Manifesto for a New Medicine: Your Guide to Healing Partnerships and the Wise Use of Alternative Therapies.*

An Unorthodox Treatment

Although she'd been told to expect a physical examination, Gibson was astonished that Gordon seemed to have no interest in her brain function. Instead, he looked at her tongue and asked her what foods she craved. He smelled her breath and gazed closely at the color of her skin. He crunched her spine in a few directions and took her pulse in a dozen places. After pinning her feet, ankles, trunk, and neck with acupuncture needles, he then left the room for half an hour, telling Gibson to breathe in through her nose and out through her mouth while the needles "brought her energy into balance." When he returned, the doctor started his talk therapy.

"What are you afraid of?" he asked her quietly.

For years Gibson had found relief from talking with her therapist about the deepest source of her pain—her mother dying when she was a baby, her father passing her off to be raised mostly by her grandparents. But as she bristled with acupuncture needles, the familiar sadness exploded like a firework. "I said, 'Loss,' and burst into tears," says Gibson, who had never put much stock in acupuncture. "Afterward I felt great."

To Gordon, Gibson's tabletop catharsis was not surprising; acupuncture often helps people express their emotions, he says, though he's unsure why. But even if this outburst would ease her feelings for a few days, he explained to Gibson, a more permanent hedge against illness required other steps: meditation to quiet her mind, exercise to make her less tense, and a short fast followed by dietary changes to improve her digestion and lower her weight. Once she transformed her physical reality, he said, her state of mind would eventually follow.

Primed for some sort of lifestyle makeover, Gibson threw herself into the program. At the psychiatrist's direction, she began taking four varieties of Chinese herbs and went back for monthly acupuncture and talk therapy sessions. Climbing the subway escalator every day on her way to work gave her more energy. After a week of eating only grapes, she limited herself to fruit and uncooked vegetables for two weeks, then to vegetables, fruit, fish, chicken, and rice. (Dairy triggered her asthma and wheat inflamed her stomach, Gordon thought, so both were ruled out, as was soda pop.)

Results came quickly. The lighter diet calmed her indigestion, and within weeks her asthma weakened its grasp on her lungs. She also started shedding pounds. And, as Gordon had promised, this physical improvement gave her a psychological lift. "I looked better. I felt terrific," she says. "I got a lot sharper."

Four years into Gordon's holistic ministrations and now fully in charge of her health, Gibson says she would never go back to the drugs that once seemed her defense against despair. "It's like my entire essence has changed."

Antidepressants

Jim Gordon makes his argument at a surprising time. After centuries of floundering, psychiatry has finally discovered a simple, effective weapon against depression, and it's the very pills he says patients don't need.

Studies show that antidepressants supply significant short-term

relief in seven of ten cases. More impressive, the drugs can often control serious, chronic depression such as that suffered by Helen Gibson.
A five-year study by University of Pittsburgh psychologist Ellen Frank
found that people who take medication prophylactically—who stay
on the drugs even after they start feeling better—cut their chances of
a relapse by 85 percent. Given results like these, it's no wonder many
psychiatrists now view their job largely as putting patients on drugs,
fiddling with brands and dosages to lessen side effects, and deciding
how long a patient should stay on the medication.

How do these drugs work? Some scientists theorize that depressed
people have less of the brain chemicals serotonin, dopamine, and
norepinephrine, which interact with nerve synapses to keep thought
processes steady. Antidepressants may serve as a kind of dam, keeping
more of these chemicals pooled around the synapses so that less is
reabsorbed into nearby brain tissue. But David Dunner, a psychiatrist
at the University of Washington's Center for Anxiety and Depression,
acknowledges that no one understands exactly how the pills affect
the brain. "We don't know the precise mechanism of depression
either," Dunner says. "So I tell my patients that even if I don't know
how they work, they've been studied and they do work."

The Need for More than Drugs

Yet lost in the excitement over drug treatment is a simple truth. For
many people with depression, drugs aren't the whole answer. For
starters, 30 percent of sufferers find the drugs totally ineffective. Doctors might have to try several drugs over many months to discover
one that works at all. Side effects, including diarrhea, drowsiness,
insomnia, impotence, constipation, and panic attacks, can make it
difficult to stay on a drug. Finally, as Gibson discovered, even the
drugs that work for you may not work indefinitely.

People searching for something better often turn up at alternative
medical practices. In a Harvard Medical School survey of people who
had seen a doctor or psychiatrist for depression in 1990, a third said
they'd also tried one or more unconventional therapies, among them
meditation and dietary supplements. Nearly 15 percent had visited an
herbalist, a chiropractor, or another nontraditional practitioner for
their illness. Gordon says a typical patient comes to him after years of
off-and-on antidepressant treatment. Most have been frustrated by
the drugs' uncertain results or daunting side effects. And nearly all, he
says, benefit from a different approach.

"I have never seen anyone transformed by Prozac," he says. "I've
seen people feel better, but cocaine makes you feel better, too. Why
not find wholeness your own way? Why not find wholeness?"

Gordon isn't opposed to antidepressants; a few of his patients stay
on previous prescriptions. But he is certain that his patients face a
deeper challenge than can be met by simply popping pills. He encour-

ages them to accept that challenge and tries to give them some tools, he says, to replace drugs. "When people are not dependent on medication and don't suffer the side effects of medication," he says, "they not only feel better, they feel better about themselves."

Sophia Jones (the name has been changed), for instance. Now 29, she was diagnosed with diabetes at the age of four, had her first panic attacks at 12, started seeing a therapist at 16, was hospitalized for bulimia at 18, and spent much of the next decade bouncing between doctors, institutions, and medications. Hers is obviously a difficult case, and her symptoms were often impervious to antidepressants. Prozac, Jones says, made her feel "sedated and nervous at the same time." But after she traded her pills for Gordon's regime of herbs, yoga, and acupuncture, she found reason to be encouraged—for the first time. "Before I spent so much energy feeling bad I didn't have the energy to do normal things," she says. "Now I've got this foundation of health, and I've got ground to stand on. I feel like I'm getting my life back."

Another Gordon patient, Jim Norman, is a wiry, intense epidemiologist at the National Institutes of Health. Norman earned a physics degree from the University of Alabama at the tender age of 18, but as his scientific career blossomed, his mood sank. Eventually he was diagnosed as having manic-depression. He tried for years to stabilize himself with tranquilizers, then started Gordon's regimen five years ago. Now, at 57, Norman finally feels he can control his moods without drugs. "The ups and downs still exist," he says, "but they've leveled out. The depression has lifted."

A scientist himself, Norman is not sure researchers will ever be able to explain the collective impact of the mind-body techniques Gordon uses. "It affirms things I always suspected," Norman says. "That we are affected by our whole environment, at basic levels, in ways science can't prove in a conventional way.

"It's hard to say why it works. I suppose that it could all be a placebo. But it worked for me."

Is Experimenting Worth the Risk?

In Seattle, where wet, gloomy winters make depression all too common a problem, David Dunner responds to talk of holistic, drug-free psychiatry as if someone's asked his medical opinion of eating glass. Considering that 15 percent of the people suffering from severe depression eventually kill themselves, the University of Washington psychiatrist says, using unproven treatments may have tragic repercussions. "I think these treatments can be dangerous," he says.

More explicit is Florida psychiatrist Mark Gold, author of *The Good News About Depression*, who worries that patients who experiment with unconventional treatments may put themselves at a sharply raised risk for chronic depression. He paints a scenario in which

someone having her first bout of depression forgoes prompt drug
therapy in favor of alternative treatments, then finds the regimen
isn't enough to prevent a relapse. "With each episode that's not treated with drugs, depression becomes less likely to be successfully treated," Gold says. Studies show that nearly 50 percent of people who
have one relapse and 90 percent of those who have two relapses can
expect to have more.

That's why most psychiatrists' biggest concern about antidepressants is not overuse but underuse. Only one-third of the 17.6 million
Americans who suffer a serious depression every year get medication.
If all depressed people were given antidepressants, the doctors say,
thousands of the 35,000 Americans who commit suicide each year
could be saved. Indeed, many psychiatrists hope everyone will some-
day accept the National Alliance for Research on Schizophrenia and
Depression's slogan—A Flaw in Chemistry, Not Character—as gospel.
In that ideal world, they say, giving antidepressants to the depressed
will be as obvious a call as giving insulin to a diabetic. "You can't have
a mood change without a chemical change in the brain," Gold says,
and drugs are the only reliable method.

But scratch the surface, and most psychiatrists will acknowledge
that other methods can also steady misfiring brain chemicals. Talk
therapy, after all, is still considered a standard treatment, presumably
because it, too, can bring about positive changes in the brain. Many
psychiatrists encourage their patients to start exercising or lose some
weight to ease their depression. And few doctors would disagree that
eating a healthier diet can make patients feel better. Gordon reports
that many of his patients, including Helen Gibson, were referred to
him by doctors seeking a professional with a nutrition background to
help their patients improve their eating habits.

Still, given that any physician can write a prescription for Prozac
that will work in most cases, even open-minded doctors advise a cautious approach to alternatives. One worry is that there are few doctors
with training in both conventional and alternative medicine, especially ones with Gordon's apparent gift for changing patients' lives. In
the hands of a lesser healer or, worse, a quack, patients like Gibson
could easily tumble into a pattern of relapse and despair. Another
concern is that it's nearly impossible to make studies of treatments
such as acupuncture or meditation—much less a complicated, varied
program like Gordon's—conform to the kinds of strictly controlled
studies that have upheld the value of antidepressant medicine.

Alternatives Deserve a Look

Despite these difficulties, reliable studies of alternatives are starting to
be done, and some have been quite encouraging. Such results, combined with the less-than-flawless record of antidepressants, virtually
guarantee more research into holistic treatment for depression, says

Dan Oren, a former program chief at the National Institute of Mental Health and now chief of the mood disorders program at Yale University's veterans medical center. "Nothing breeds success like success," he says.

Helen Gibson is glad she didn't wait for definitive research to confirm the value of a holistic approach. After decades of using pills to overcome her harrowing feelings, she says, she's thankful that the dietary and other suggestions Gordon offered gave her a measure of control over her illness. "I inherited my depression, and it will always be with me," Gibson says. "But it's manageable. I feel like I got balanced, mentally and physically. I feel more cleansed, which is a silly word, but it's true."

Oren isn't discounting stories like Gibson's. "I'll lose my curiosity about alternatives," says the researcher, "when we come up with the perfect drug."

HERBAL RELIEF FOR DEPRESSION

Benedict Carey

> Saint-John's-wort, a yellow-flowering herb, has received much attention for its natural effectiveness in relieving depression. In the following selection, Benedict Carey, a contributing editor for *Health* magazine, describes the surge in popularity of this humble herb. According to Carey, various scientific studies have reported the success rates of Saint-John's-wort in offering relief for sufferers of chronic depression as well as for those who experience milder forms of the illness. While the herb can be beneficial for many, warns Carey, Saint-John's-wort is still a form of medication and should not be taken without care.

It's happening again: the pill swallowing and tea brewing, the patter of pungent brown droplets falling into water, all the sacraments of that recurring ritual in which we attempt to better our lives using the latest natural healing sensation. This time the promise of redemption comes in the form of a yellow-flowering herb Europeans have used for centuries against a variety of nerve and mood disorders. Since late 1996, when the trusted *British Medical Journal* published an analysis of 23 German studies concluding that Saint-John's-wort is effective for certain forms of depression, the herb has been big business on this side of the Atlantic as well, with sales up more than tenfold.

"All sorts of people are coming in and asking for it, from grandmothers all the way down to teenagers," says Johnny Maccini, who works at Whole Foods Market in West Los Angeles. Indeed, a rash of breathless media reports sparked such demand that suppliers have had to scramble to keep up.

Because Saint-John's-wort has gotten the same good-for-whatever-ails-you buzz that surrounded previous natural elixirs like melatonin and DHEA, even people who aren't depressed are taking it, hoping they've found an antidote to life's garden-variety ups and downs. ("People say Saint-John's-wort is great for when you're stuck in traffic," says Maccini.)

The herb's principal constituency, though, is a far less frivolous group. A 30-year-old San Francisco journalist, for example, says Saint-John's-wort helped her through a painful and protracted breakup. "I just wanted to stop waking up every morning feeling like the world was going to end," she says. "I took it for a couple of months and stopped when I felt I didn't need it."

A 50-year-old graphic designer in Oakland, California, says he suffered weeklong bouts of despair almost every month until he started taking the herb. "It has evened me out so I don't feel the real lows anymore," he says. "The other day I learned that a book I had worked on wasn't selling—something that would have set me off a year ago. Well, not this time. I feel the Saint-John's-wort has given me a real emotional resiliency."

If you're a skeptical sort, such anecdotal evidence may set off alarms. Miracle potions come and go in the natural healing racket, after all, and depressives need false hope like they need a death in the family.

Legitimated by Scientists

Yet many establishment scientists are treating Saint-John's-wort with respect because there's reputable research to back up the testimonials. The herb has been examined in more than 40 scientific studies of mild to moderate depression, almost all of them done in Germany.

Combining 13 of the best ones analyzed in the *British Medical Journal*, researchers found that 55 percent of patients taking Saint-John's-wort improved their scores on standard measures of depression, compared with 22 percent who improved on dummy pills. Saint-John's-wort not only helped people feel happier but rid them of moderate depression's physical symptoms, including insomnia, lack of appetite, and fatigue. "I think it's fair to say that the evidence so far is pretty good for small first-time studies," says Jane Steinberg, a psychologist at the National Institutes of Health (NIH).

Also encouraging is the experience of millions in Germany who've found Saint-John's-wort safe and easy to take. It's the most popular antidepressant there, as ubiquitous as aspirin, and it outsells Prozac seven to one. It has far fewer side effects than the standard drugs: Of 3,250 patients taking Saint-John's-wort for a month during a 1994 study, fewer than 3 percent suffered dry mouth, gastric problems, or dizziness. (Most users of synthetic antidepressants experience these or other side effects, usually with greater intensity.) Nor does the herb react badly with alcohol, cheese, pickles, and other foods to cause the migraine-like reaction common in people taking older drugs called MAO inhibitors.

The one exotic risk linked with Saint-John's-wort has shown itself only in animals: Light-skinned cattle feeding on the shrub become very sensitive to ultraviolet light and suffer severe sunburns. But so far light-skinned people haven't reported similar problems.

Pharmacologists are at a loss to explain how Saint-John's-wort does its work. Because it produces the same kinds of side effects as Prozac and its chemical cousins, researchers assume that the herb, too, slows the breakdown of the brain chemical serotonin, low levels of which are thought to be associated with depression. Yet in a few experiments Saint-John's-wort has shown broader activity, also altering the concentrations of other neurotransmitters like dopamine and norepinephrine.

"We've tried to understand it by comparing it to the antidepressants we know, fitting it into the boxes we already have on the shelf, and so far it doesn't fit," says Benedetto Vitiello, a pharmacologist at the National Institute of Mental Health. "There are many ingredients that could be active, and there may be some completely new process at work."

Whatever that process is, it's intriguing enough to have prompted the NIH to undertake the largest, longest-running study of the herb to date. And it's not just the Office of Alternative Medicine (OAM) that's involved. Considered by some the New Age adolescent of the NIH family, the OAM is being joined for this study by two distinguished cosponsors, the National Institute of Mental Health and the Office of Dietary Supplements, giving the investigation added clout.

In Spring 1998 researchers will recruit 336 patients with moderate depression at several clinics across the country. Every day for eight weeks the patients will take either a dummy pill, a Prozac-style antidepressant, or a standard 900-milligram capsule of Saint-John's-wort. (This form was chosen because the teas and tinctures sold in health food stores don't deliver reliable doses.) Patients who do well on the herb will be followed for an additional 18 weeks.

The researchers hope to clarify how the herb measures up to the newer antidepressants—the German studies compared Saint-John's-wort only with older drugs—and whether continued use can prevent relapses. Results are expected in 2001.

Take Caution Nonetheless

In the meantime, psychiatrists who prescribe the herb have some advice for anyone who plans to experiment with Saint-John's-wort or is doing so already. Don't diagnose yourself, they say; consult a physician to find out how serious your depression is.

Of course, that detracts from the herb's do-it-yourself appeal. But lost in the hubbub over Saint-John's-wort is the fact that it's by no means a cure, even for mild conditions. Only 15 percent of the people included in the 13 *British Medical Journal* studies, for instance, enjoyed complete remission of their symptoms. One hallmark of depression is that those who have it often can't clearly assess the seriousness of their condition, and for anyone with severe depression—marked by constant crying, thoughts of suicide, overwhelming feelings of worthlessness or guilt—self-medicating with Saint-John's-wort could be downright dangerous. The herb has never been formally tested in such cases, and psychiatrists who have prescribed it for more troubled patients say that it doesn't seem to bring them relief.

"It's possible that Saint-John's-wort could become a real first-line treatment for millions of people who need help and aren't getting it," says Steinberg of the NIH. "Obviously, that's what you hope for. But if it gives people a false sense of security, prevents them from seeing somebody about their problems, then it could do harm."

Another caveat: Do not mix Saint-John's-wort with other antidepressants. Doing so could lead to a harmful rise in blood pressure or to a condition called serotonin syndrome. Mild cases of the latter are marked by sweating, agitation, an upset stomach, jerky muscles, and insomnia, while severe cases can bring on seizures, coma, even death.

Finally, if you're not depressed, don't expect Saint-John's-wort to float you through a bad day or week. Most people who take it don't notice any difference at all for the first month or longer, and even then the change is typically subtle.

As it should be. An instant cure for the bad days would only make us forget what the truly good ones look like.

LISTENING TO THE SYSTEM

Peggy Papp

Writing from the point of view of a therapist, Peggy Papp discusses the intricacies of personal problems that professionals should consider when treating depressed patients. Papp explains that social systems indirectly contribute to symptoms of depression. A depressed patient's role in a relationship is often established partially by hierarchies of gender or race as set forth by cultural guidelines, according to the author, and may significantly affect the course of treatment. Therefore, she emphasizes, the influence of social systems in a patient's life deserve careful consideration during the process of talk therapy. Papp is a faculty member of the Ackerman Institute for the Family in New York, where she is the director of the Depression in Context Project. She is coauthor of *The Invisible Web: Gender Patterns in Relationships* and the author of *The Process of Change*.

Over the years, I have watched a parade of treatments for depression mesmerize the field, promising so much but ultimately failing to help many clients get free of their distress. In spite of all our efforts and all the things we have learned, the causes of and means to alleviate depression often remain enigmatic. It's as if we have all the pieces in front of us, but we still, somehow, haven't assembled them into a comprehensive, multidimensional treatment for depression. Our problem is that each of our theories seems helpful in some cases, and not so helpful in others, which has meant, for many clients, a trial-and-error experience in therapy. One man spent 22 years in every kind of therapy imaginable, from cognitive, to family systems, to individual psychoanalysis, and nothing seemed to budge his great weight of hopelessness and pessimism—not Prozac, therapy, lithium, homeopathy or acupuncture. Finally, a new physician on his health plan discovered he suffered from a chronic thyroid condition that, when treated, immediately lifted his depression.

How do we assess what kind of depression someone has—whether it is caused by the hormonal changes of childbirth, the pain of divorce or the feeling of being a person of color once again passed over for a

From Peggy Papp, "Listening to the System." This article first appeared in the *Family Therapy Networker* (January/February 1997) and is excerpted here with permission.

promotion in favor of a white colleague? We now know that our brain chemistry changes when we are depressed, but did the brain changes come after some precipitating event? Depression remains one of the most difficult conditions to treat because of the vast range of factors that may be creating and maintaining it. Unfortunately, our training rarely prepares us to address the multidimensionality of depression, arming us only with one, maybe two, models for approaching the problem.

Recently, the conventional wisdom has declared that depression is biological and genetically derived, but while the promise of Prozac and other sophisticated chemical interventions seems very alluring, this explanation ignores too many questions that systems thinkers need to be asking. "Is it only biology that makes women twice as prone to depression as men?" "What about the role played by stressful childhood events, life experience and current relationships in our clients' depression?"

In social work school, I learned that depression was repressed rage. Sigmund Freud, in *Mourning and Melancholia*, illustrated the links between depression and anger turned inward, and taught that the ventilation of repressed feelings is the key to mental health. Cognitive-behavioral approaches, which have been researched more than any other approach to depression, have been found to be as effective in the treatment of depression as antidepressants. While a cognitive therapist who helps a depressed client to stop generalizing from one setback—a poor grade on a math test, for example—to his or her entire life—"I fail at everything"—has certainly done that client a service, yet no attention has been paid to the client's relationships and systemic connections.

At the time I began studying family therapy, depression was a neglected area in our field. Occasionally, someone would refer to a depressed family member as "the symptom-bearer," relegating him or her to the same status as the "acting out child." Strategic therapists Jay Haley and Cloé Madanes taught that depression served a function in the system. They related depression to the skewed hierarchy in the marital relationship, believing that the one-down spouse gained power by acting helpless and depressed. Although I never saw depression that way, the idea that depression occurs in a systemic context struck a chord with me.

Humans Shape Emotions

By 1991, I could see that therapists' search for the one true cure for depression was overshadowing what we, in the family therapy field have always known: that human systems play a powerful role in shaping our emotional states. Along with therapists Gloria Klein, Paul Feinberg and Jeffrey Seibel, I started the Ackerman Institute's Depression in Context Project to try to bring a systemic perspective to the treatment of depression, and to explore how issues involving gender, race, class and sexual orientation can catalyze its onset. One trainee asked me how, as therapists, we could possibly keep track of so many elements in therapy—all that, plus clients' work situations, biological predisposition, multigenerational family histories, distressing life events and more. My answer to her was that we would have to let the families lead us. Learning to listen to the system and determine the multiple influences on the depressed client has been the mainstay of our method and provides us with many more therapeutic options.

What follows are some of the clinical speculations and methods that have emerged from the first five years of our project seeing chronically depressed clients and their families who have been referred by therapists and psychiatrists after multiple suicide attempts, hospitalizations, rounds of medications and therapies. Although I am presenting the highlights of certain of our cases, I don't want to paint a picture of a smooth ride. With some of these clients, we have had to hold our breath the whole time, knowing they have been suicidal and could easily become so again. Therapy with depressed clients is nerve-wracking work because their ties to life are so tenuous and easily snapped. Often, we had to go on faith that focusing on the available support systems was really making a difference.

No two cases involving depression are ever alike, and there are no cookie-cutter solutions We have found that in every case the marital partnership has enormous potential to become a truly healing relationship.

Women who lose their voice in relationships often become depressed, and the best antidote is being heard.

When Lucy and George, both age 38, were referred to us by her psychiatrist, Lucy had already been hospitalized seven times for depression—twice for attempted suicides—and she had been on an array of antidepressants for more than a decade. A frail-looking woman who had given up her doctoral studies in community organizing when pregnant with her first child, Lucy spoke in a faint whisper. She and George, an attorney who had recently become a partner in his New York City law firm, had been married for 15 years. They had two sons, ages 5 and 8. Lucy had undergone electroconvulsive therapy (ECT) treatments twice, with no perceptible change. She had been in individual therapy since age 12, after her father abandoned the family, leaving her mother to raise and financially support Lucy and an older brother. George reported that Lucy often could not get out of bed. She suffered from sudden and frequent crying spells— which she demonstrated throughout the first few sessions. She was withdrawn, as if she were shrinking into herself. George sat looking apprehensive and defensive.

When we asked Lucy what she thought was causing her depression, it was hard to hear her response. After many long pauses, she told us her depression might be due to "the cold temperature in the marriage." She became slightly more animated when we invited her to say more. "My husband blames my depression for the problems in the marriage," she whispered, adding that she believed there was a connection between the problems in the marriage and the depression. Lucy felt there was a tremendous emotional distance between herself and George, and she felt hopeless about ever improving the relationship. "We are immune to help," she told us. "Nothing can save us." When we asked her what made the relationship so hopeless, she cited the long hours George worked and the way they disagreed about budgeting their money—George was more worried about their spending and constantly policed her household expenses. The idea of being stuck with George in their same-old relationship made her feel trapped. "I would leave him if I could afford to," she said in one session. "But what would I do? Where would I go?" George wasn't surprised to learn she had been thinking of leaving him. He had warned her that if she ever did try to leave him, he would use her psychiatric history against her and sue for custody of the children, even though he did not consider her an unfit mother.

No More Sounds of Silence

Psychologist Dana Crowley Jack, author of *Silencing the Self,* concluded that the best way to find out what made depressed women feel depressed was to ask them directly. What she heard again and again mirrored what we were hearing from Lucy: "I lost my voice—and myself—in the relationship." Many of our women clients have been, like Lucy, unable to trust their feelings, unable to believe they are entitled even to have feelings. They are financially and emotionally dependent on their husbands and afraid of isolation or reprisal if they express themselves openly, so they give up in despair and lapse into depression.

In the course of encouraging these women to speak about what seems so forbidden in their families and marriages, we are careful not to cast blame on their husbands. We view the husbands as an essential resource and focus on their potential to help their wives, something the husbands feel they have failed to do during the long years of depression. This failure causes them tremendous pain because it is so important to them, as it is for most men, to feel competent. We convey a sense of confidence in their ability to do something that will make a difference, sympathizing with their anger, frustration and despair when their efforts fail, acknowledging their fortitude and commitment and appreciating their successes. In the process of helping the depressed client overcome his or her depression, we are helping couples unravel the stranglehold that the depression has assumed in both their lives so that they can find healthier and happier ways to be together.

Nonetheless, on hearing his wife's complaints about their marriage, George grew understandably defensive. He explained to us that he had tried and tried to help Lucy and was continually frustrated when nothing worked. He tried to offer her concrete, logical suggestions—typical of what most husbands do. They problem-solve, offering advice, such as "increase your medication," "get involved in work," "think positive thoughts." Well-meaning but misfiring, George did everything except the one thing Lucy wanted, which was for him to listen to her thoughts, feelings and complaints about the relationship. And if she did try to raise one of the hot issues at home, he would feel overwhelmed and either explode in a rage or leave the room.

Making Progress

Addressing the power imbalance in the couple relationship and creating a sense of safety for depressed wives to express the thoughts and feelings they have suppressed is a key piece of our work. Lucy had a tendency to back down and retreat whenever George got angry. Before our eyes, she would wither and fade. We encouraged her to keep going, hold onto what she was saying, not be intimidated. One issue that came up was George's drinking problem. He practically sputtered in surprise when she said this to us—her voice having grown noticeably stronger and clearer over the three weeks of therapy. George glowered at her as she described his nightly withdrawal into an alcoholic cave. She talked about how confronting years of this hidden drinking, unable to tell anyone, left her feeling emotionally abandoned and alone. George, his face beet red, felt betrayed by her disclosure. After he calmed down, we talked about what effect he thought his drinking had on the family. He acknowledged that it was having a detrimental effect on the marriage, eventually conceding that he was secretly worried that, like his mother, he might be an alcoholic. He and Lucy negotiated that he would limit himself to two glasses of wine a night and if he couldn't do that, he would go to Alcoholics Anonymous (AA).

George followed through on his promise and cut his drinking down dramatically over the next few months, until finally he wasn't drinking at all. To Lucy, this made an enormous difference because she felt he had heard her and that he valued the relationship enough to do something that was so difficult for him. Her feelings of warmth and affection toward him became easier to express—feelings that had been cut off and withheld for many years. Lucy had also visibly changed, now coming in to our office with more energy, sitting up straight, speaking in an audible voice, looking at George when she spoke more often than not, even smiling once or twice. While she still suffered from occasional relapses into her depression, she had become more assertive, was able to leave the house and take care of things like shopping and car pooling. She even began to get active in the community after being asked by the neighborhood association to help them organize a voter registration outreach effort. Her lifelong habit of feeling hopelessly defeated still emerged during crises, but she now had other ways of coping besides silencing herself.

Meeting Expectations of Gender

Gender roles and beliefs often serve to influence and maintain depression in clients.

Delving into something as seemingly abstract as gender roles and beliefs can seem at best extraneous, at worst the imposition of the therapist's own political agenda in the therapy. But we have discovered that these deep-seated beliefs play an enormously important role in both the onset and maintenance of depression in all our clients, and talking about them often gets to the heart of how they make meaning of their lives. For women, gender stereotypes that might affect depression include the belief that they have to be beautiful, slender, sexy; inhibit their anger; assume responsibility for the physical and emotional well-being for everyone in the family; put their own needs second and accept the blame for anything that goes wrong. For men, the stereotypes might include that they must achieve status, money and prestige; appear to be bold and self-confident; take charge of every situation; and, above all, never to reveal any signs of weakness or vulnerability.

To assess what role these beliefs, and the meanings ascribed to these beliefs, play in our clients' depression, we ask each family member to fill out a questionnaire that focuses on these issues. It queries the kinds of messages they received from their parents about being male or female; how closely they feel they have fulfilled those expectations; whether there were any contradictory messages; and how they might have rebelled against or conformed to those expectations. We also ask what effect those expectations might be having on current relationships, on their sense of power, privilege and independence. In the process, clients begin to develop for themselves an understanding of how these gender roles have influenced their depression by forcing them to ascribe to beliefs and norms that might not fit them.

Gender Roles Are Passed Down

Charles and Loretta, an African-American couple in their early sixties, came to therapy because Charles was hospitalized for an episode of depression and had become so immobilized he was unable to continue on his job. When we asked him why he thought he was depressed, he said it was related to work. He had just been transferred to a new department and promoted to a high-level managerial position, and he felt extremely anxious. As a child, his father had told him that to succeed as a black man, he had to be three times as good as a white person. His striving and constant assessment of how he was doing habitually cut him off from any kind of collaborative relationship with his colleagues because he felt he had to be perfect, to know everything and to never show a moment's weakness. This was virtually impossible in the type of job to which he was now assigned, where working on a team was essential for getting the work done. He felt self-conscious and highly vulnerable, which made him anxious and then depressed. Our first few sessions focused on lowering his unrealistically high expectations of himself so he would be able to return to work.

After filling out his questionnaire, Charles explored the beliefs passed to him from his father about being a successful black man. His father had been raised in poverty. After Charles's mother died when he was a teenager, his father struggled to raise the children, drilling into them the idea that they had to be self-reliant. Manhood, Charles had been taught, meant sacrificing your own needs, your own life, to provide for your family. Charles began to realize that, as he put it, he had been "in a driven state for the last number of years." He had been going to night school to get his MBA, working 11-hour days and he had not taken any weekends off in months. He could not remember his last vacation and he still felt he was not doing enough to both get ahead and put his family on firmer financial footing.

Having no time to devote to his family, he had become cut off from their lives. When his son decided to drop out of college to pursue a career as an artist, Charles's depression intensified. But during a therapy session with his children and wife, he finally understood what his son was saying to him. "I am afraid if I graduate college and become a lawyer or doctor, I will have to be like you," his son said. "I want more of a life for myself. I can't be a man the way you are modeling it for me." Both children felt they didn't know their dad. He never talked about his dreams or his doubts or expressed any feelings. In therapy, they began to ask questions about his life and childhood. He told them stories about his college days, his love of the violin and his prowess at football, which he had given up to work on getting better grades. His opening up wasn't just therapeutic for the children; Charles told us, "This is such a relief to know this is not dangerous to talk about, that my family is supportive and I can share these things."

Our therapy team has a basic belief that men are perfectly capable of expressing their feelings and being emotionally available and supportive. This perspective prevents us from being immobilized, as are many of our colleagues, by the belief that, "Oh well, that's the way men are." We also believe that women are capable of asserting themselves, thinking logically and taking charge of their lives. The heart of our work is challenging and uncovering those gender stereotypes that are strangling and impoverishing for both men and women.

When depressed clients can openly discuss previously unspoken larger system issues—such as racism or sexism—that make them feel powerless and attack their self-esteem, the depression may lift.

Depression is universally described as a profound disturbance of mood connected with a negative self-image. Terms such as "lack of self-esteem," "low self-image" and "feelings of worthlessness" are used over and over in the literature on depression. Self-esteem doesn't exist in a vacuum but in a relational and social context, which is profoundly influenced not only by gender stereotypes and norms, but also by discrimination on the basis of race, class, sexual orientation and other areas where one is made to feel less-than. Of course, not all people who face such discrimination suffer from full-blown depression or even low self-esteem. but in combination with other stressors and predispositions, it can play a large part in affecting the depression. Many therapists feel confounded, however, about how to work on these broad social issues since none of us can wave our wands and magically eradicate something as embedded as society's racism. In our project. we have discovered that what does help is, once again, bringing the issue out into the open. Even if the therapist can't change the situation, we can help the depressed person avoid personalizing it and letting it corrode his or her self-esteem.

The discussion with Charles and Loretta about how gender beliefs and stereotypes played out in their lives led to an unprecedented conversation in their family about racism. Charles mused that his father had believed that he would have to be nearly perfect to protect himself from the unfairness of racism, and even perfection would not be enough. The deeply embedded beliefs and messages, as well as examples of the powerlessness of African Americans when they came face-to-face with racism, had been with him throughout his life. He watched his father's fear of losing his job when a new white supervisor came on and threatened all the black workers. He wondered if his rejection from two graduate programs was on account of his race. He feared all the time for the safety of his children—particularly his son—and decided to work even harder to make more money to send them to private school to try to protect them. His son, explaining why he had dropped out of college, said, "I want to be loved for who I am, not for what I do." This was a whole new concept to his father, and we spent a lot of time helping this family understand what they valued and how they coped with living in a racist society as people of color. At the end of therapy, Charles told us, "I couldn't be loved by the white society for who I am, but I am learning that I can be loved for who I am by my family."

Making Connections

Getting depressed men connected with their wives is a powerful intervention to move them out of their depression.

Everything seemed fine with Charles, so we were surprised when he suffered a relapse. He came back to therapy and reported that one of the symptoms he was suffering from was an inability to fall asleep. A therapist on the team asked him, "What do you lie awake thinking," and Charles answered, "Maybe I worry about my wife."

After a number of sessions with Charles, Loretta and their children, this was the first mention anyone in their family had made about the recent diagnosis that Loretta's breast cancer might be recurring. Her doctor had found a lump in her breast and ordered a biopsy. When she had a mastectomy six years earlier, she had gone to the hospital alone, not wanting their two high-school-age children to take time off from school and not wanting Charles to miss work. She now kept telling Charles, "Don't worry about me. I'll take care of myself. I don't want you to get all upset because you might get more depressed." Loretta was a strong woman who had devoted her life to taking care of others. When she filled out our questionnaire about gender beliefs, it was clear that being the strong one and not needing any support from others was who she expected she would have to be as a black woman.

Loretta dismissed the notion that she might need someone to lean on. We asked Charles if he planned to accompany her to the hospital this time. He said he would if she wanted him to. Loretta protectively said it was hard for him to deal with her condition because his mother had died of cancer. We suggested that since Loretta had spent her life taking care of others' needs, she had forgotten how to ask for what she needed. We asked Charles, "Would it be possible for you to mobilize some of your strength and resources to help her through this ordeal?" Charles said it was difficult for him to give his wife support and attention when he was in his depressed state, but he would try.

Opening Up

Loretta began the following session by saying that she had awakened in the middle of the night from a horrible dream. "It was the first thing that signaled me how afraid I was," she told us. In her panic, she cried out and Charles responded by holding her in his arms and comforting her. It was the first time the couple had embraced in 10 years. Loretta said, "This kind of intimacy from him is rare. It meant a lot to me because I was petrified." It proved to be a transforming experience for Charles, who told us, with tears in his eyes, "I can't explain it. I felt a strong love that was brought about by a need for touch." Being needed and making an emotional connection with his wife gave Charles the feeling of being strong and effective in an area in which men often don't feel competent.

Charles's new emotional openness spilled into his work situation. He told his co-workers about his wife's condition—he had never shared any personal information before. They responded by sending Loretta flowers, which made Charles feel like an accepted and well-liked member of the work team. We were all greatly relieved to learn that Loretta's breast tumor was benign.

Helping the Self by Helping Others

In other cases, we have used this same intervention coaching depressed husbands to develop empathy toward their wives by focusing on their needs, and it has never failed to have a positive effect on the depression. Of the many depressed husbands we have coached in this way, we have never heard one say he had nothing to give to his wife. Why does this work? Our team began theorizing that since all the depressed men we saw seemed completely out of touch with their own or others feelings, becoming emotionally connected with their wives was a first step in beginning to feel. The wives of depressed men, we discovered, always appreciate their involvement and support since they often have had to shoulder 100 percent of the responsibility to keep the family going. Getting the husbands to focus on their wives' needs isn't about getting them to take out the garbage, it's about coaching them into a state of empathy. If they begin to imagine what it's like for their wives, emotionally, they come out of their cocoon of disconnection.

The conventional wisdom in our field is that men have to get in touch with their own feelings first, before they can be there emotionally for anyone else. But we are challenging this much-cherished notion by asking husbands to be there for their wives. We have found that it is possible for a depressed husband to do something for someone else despite being depressed, and the very act of helping can have a salutary effect on depression. . . .

Interactions Really Matter

The research has long suggested a connection between systems and depression. It has been established, for example, that the most stressful life event precipitating depression is marital conflict, which is also the single most predictable indicator of relapse. We develop and maintain our sense of ourselves through interactions with others, and if those exchanges are fraught with suffocating silences, loneliness and disconnection, self-esteem and self-image crumble. Treating depression as if it exists only in the thoughts that course through a brain, or only within the chemical washes of a body, ignores the complexities and richness of human experience. Even though I have been a family therapist for years, I continue to be amazed at the power of the family system to bring its members back into the light.

A VIRTUAL SHOULDER TO CRY ON

Laura Spinney

With the widespread use of computers and the popularity of the Internet, sufferers of depression are finding a bevy of online outlets for diagnosing and treating their illness. In the following selection, Laura Spinney explores the effectiveness of treatment through the Internet. Looking at both American and British websites, Spinney describes popular e-mail discussion groups and services for depression. She also examines the opinions and ideas of psychiatrists who are attempting to employ technology to provide medical treatment for the disorder. Spinney is a freelance journalist who frequently writes about contemporary health issues.

Friedrich Nietzsche described the thought of suicide as a great source of comfort. Had he lived in the 1990s, he might have contacted the popular Internet mailgroup *alt.suicide.holiday*, which provides users with a forum for comparing the effectiveness of various methods of self-destruction, and an open ear into which they can pour streams of anguish. Not everybody would agree that the *alt.suicide.holiday* mailgroup serves a constructive purpose, but there are now hundreds of self-help groups on the Internet offering practical and emotional support for psychological problems ranging from alcoholism through depression to schizophrenia.

That such groups exist is not entirely surprising. Pressure to cut healthcare costs is increasing throughout the developed world, and services such as long-term psychotherapy are often given a lower priority than treatments for more acute conditions. Indeed, there is more pressure than ever on psychiatric resources. A study published in the *Journal of Clinical Psychiatry* put the total cost of treating depression in the US at $43.7 billion in 1990, the same as was spent on treating coronary heart disease. Some practitioners and patients view e-mail discussion groups as an alternative source of information and support for the mentally ill, though they acknowledge it may not be as effective as professional help.

Others suggest that if e-mail and psychotherapy were found to be compatible approaches, the structured 50-minute sessions beloved of therapists could be replaced by a much more flexible medium of com-

Reprinted, with permission, from Laura Spinney, "A Virtual Shoulder to Cry On," *New Scientist*, December 9, 1995.

munication. However, to date few psychotherapists have been pre-pared to throw their weight behind the idea.

Cost is not the only obstacle to tackling mental health problems. There is also the attached social stigma. A report in the *British Medical Journal* in 1992 claimed that every year three per cent of the general population in Britain are diagnosed by general practitioners as suffer-ing from depression. The research went on to show that GPs fail to recognise roughly the same number of cases during consultations. Many more people suffering the symptoms of depression do not feel that they are sufficiently ill to visit a doctor. The report concluded that half of all cases of depression in Britain go undetected. This is borne out by figures that put the true incidence of major depression at five per cent of the population. Another estimate suggests that at least one in three people will suffer a depressive episode during their lifetime.

Robin Priest, chairman of the Defeat Depression Campaign, a joint venture by the Royal College of Psychiatrists and the Royal College of General Practitioners, says that many people with depression would rather buy a self-help book or attend an anonymous self-help group than consult their doctor. Hence the popularity of the Samaritans, the organisation set up in London in 1953 to offer anonymous emotional support to depressed and suicidal people.

Psychological Screening

While joining an online discussion group can offer similar anonymi-ty, some researchers believe that computers could have a more far-reaching role. Services that use the Internet to provide users with advice and information on psychological matters already exist. There have also been studies into the effectiveness of techniques such as psychological screening over the telephone, where users are given a series of questions that enable them to assess for themselves whether or not their symptoms merit a visit to the doctor. Similar programs that display the questions on computer screens have also been tested. And some psychiatrists have begun to investigate the potential for using computers to achieve more detailed diagnoses and even to administer treatment for certain mental disorders.

One of the more high-profile uses of the Internet in helping people with mental health problems is the Samaritans' e-mail scheme, which was piloted in 1994 and is now in operation at five branches. The scheme, which allows anyone with access to e-mail to send a message to one of the volunteers, had its busiest period in the summer of 1995 when many students were under pressure from exams. Leo Leibovici, e-mail befriending coordinator for the Samaritans in Britain, estimates that of the 1100 e-mail contacts made in the first year of the scheme, a quarter were received in the summer of 1995.

E-mail is seen as an extension of the services provided by the organisation, which has offered a "sympathetic ear" to anyone who contacts it in person, by letter or by telephone, since its formation. "Trawling through the Usenet groups, things like *alt.suicide.holiday* and *alt.support.depression*, and reading those messages, we realised that there were a lot of people on the Net who could certainly benefit from talking to the Samaritans and perhaps were not able to or willing to do so by other means," says Leibovici.

E-Mail Ease

He points out that the e-mail service has opened up the Samaritans' support network to one of the groups most vulnerable to depression—men aged 18 to 24. Between 1982 and 1992 the suicide rate in this group rose by 85 per cent in England and Wales, far outstripping the rate among women in the same age group.

Among telephone callers to the Samaritans, 25 per cent express suicidal thoughts. During the first six months of the e-mail project, however, 75 per cent of those who made contact admitted that they had considered killing themselves. Young men often find it difficult to express their feelings verbally, says Leibovici, because they do not consider it "the thing to do". Also, students may find it easier to find a terminal from which they can send confidential messages than a phone which isn't in a public place. Many universities and colleges now provide students with e-mail accounts.

Seeing your problems expressed as words typed on a computer screen can be therapeutic in itself, says Leibovici. But doesn't the impersonality of a screen deter people from expressing their true feelings? On the contrary, says Leibovici, with e-mail there is no small talk: "Somebody will come straight in and say 'I'm feeling like shit. I want to die, tell me why I shouldn't'. And that's it. Often that would take half an hour to an hour [for someone to admit] on the phone." It is also less easy for the volunteers to make assumptions about the age, gender or nationality of a caller. This is a good thing, says Leibovici, because Samaritans are encouraged to be completely nonjudgmental.

Word Perfect

The Samaritans' e-mail volunteers are already trained to deal with callers over the telephone, and they receive about 12 hours extra tuition for e-mail work, mostly in the use of written language. "It's different from the phone in that you've got longer to think about what you're putting down," says Leibovici. "You don't have to give an instant reaction. But you've got to bear in mind that the caller who receives the message is also going to have a very long time to look at it. So you have to be very careful that you don't put something that could be misunderstood."

There are two alternatives for those wanting to get in touch with the Samaritans electronically. Either they can e-mail *jo@samaritans.org* direct, or they can send their message via an anonymous server in

Helsinki, Finland. The latter strips off their e-mail address, replaces it with an unidentifiable number and then automatically relays the message to the Samaritans, which has no way of telling from whom or where it came. A Samaritans volunteer can then reply via the same route.

Although it can be slow—sometimes a message takes three hours to get through—the anonymous route is popular, accounting for about 40 per cent of the e-mail contacts says Leibovici. And the security that it offers has prompted many people to contact the organisation who might otherwise have felt inhibited. Another advantage of e-mail is that time zones no longer matter. Leibovici estimates that half the electronic postbag now comes from overseas.

Computers Allow Self-Evaluation

The Samaritans describes its work as befriending and, as with the organisation's other services, volunteers do not offer counselling or advice. There are, however, a number of organisations and research groups that have looked at using computers and the Internet to administer more active forms of therapy. Some studies suggest that computer-mediated diagnosis and analysis have a place in psychotherapy. A pilot study in 1994 at the University of Dundee in Scotland compared diagnoses made by trained psychiatrists at the State Hospital in Carstairs, Scotland, with those of a computer program designed to allow psychiatric patients to assess their own mental state, for example how angry they are.

In a group of 13 patients, most of them schizophrenic, self-evaluation using computers correlated closely with the psychiatrists' assessment. And patients found the computer program just as easy to respond to as the more conventional tests using pen and paper. Similar results were noted when the same computer-based tests were used to evaluate child psychiatric patients and elderly people suffering from dementia.

Lending Voice to the Depressed

Researchers in the US led by Lee Baer of the Consolidated Department of Psychiatry at Harvard Medical School in Massachusetts have also tried out computerised screening techniques. The difference here was that they used their system to detect clinical depression in volunteers from the general public. Their study, published in the *Journal of the American Medical Association* in June 1994, described how they used "interactive voice response", a hybrid telephone/computer system, to administer the 20-question Zung Self-Rating Depression Scale.

Volunteers were recruited from a large company that manufactures hi-tech goods, and a state university. Each site had a population of around 35 000. The researchers recruited volunteers by publishing a list of the classic symptoms of depression in employee and student magazines and newspapers. They also broadcast the list through the student radio station, posters and e-mail. If people recognised any of the symptoms in themselves, but felt that they needed advice before seeking professional help, they were encouraged to call a number and answer prerecorded questions using the buttons of a touch-tone telephone. They were asked to respond to statements such as "I have crying spells" or "I get tired for no reason" by pressing a number between one and four according to how often they experienced these feelings.

The researchers found that 70 per cent of those who participated showed at least mild depression, and 75 per cent said they found the call helpful. They concluded that interactive voice response could be an effective, confidential and low-cost diagnostic tool for depression.

The Personal Touch?

But will computers replace the experts? Priest is sceptical about computer programs replacing humans when it comes to assessing the severity of depression, because he feels that this requires the subtleties of human judgement.

Joseph Kobos, director of the counselling service at the University of Texas Health Science Centre at San Antonio is also cautious in his support for techniques such as e-mail counselling. E-mail, he says, is too limited a medium of communication to support such a relationship.

Anne Zachary, a consultant psychotherapist in London, agrees. She believes that it would be difficult to diagnose a psychological illness either by e-mail or over the phone. Without the extra information provided by tone of voice and body language it is not safe to make a diagnosis, she says.

In his book *The Psychology of Interpersonal Behaviour*, British psychologist Michael Argyle describes research which shows that body language, or nonverbal communication, can be up to five times more effective than words alone at conveying emotions or attitudes. On the other hand, he says, information can be passed on and problems solved just as well over the telephone as in face-to-face communication, provided visual materials such as maps are not needed.

Guy Fielding, a communication specialist at the Department of Communication and Information Studies at Queen Margaret College, Edinburgh, says telephone communication is actually more reliable than face-to-face communication. "It's actually more difficult to deceive over the telephone than it is face-to-face," he says. This is because most of the cues that tell you whether someone is lying are auditory. In a face-to-face situation, a listener's attention is distracted from these cues by misleading visual ones. In his view, this is why Sigmund Freud arranged his consulting room so that from where he sat at the head of the couch he was unable to make eye contact with his recumbent client.

Computer Therapists?

But can computers help patients once they have been diagnosed? In 1995, psychologists at Kaiser Permanente, a private healthcare organisation in Los Angeles, compared computer-assisted therapy in a head-to-head with a human therapist. Patients with clinical depression and anxiety were either given an hour and a half of group therapy a week, or a shorter session preceded by a session with the Therapeutic Learning Program (TLP).

TLP is a self-help computer program in which patients work through a series of menus, first to identify sources of stress and factors in their lifestyle which contribute to it, and then to work out what they could do to resolve the situation. Depression and anxiety ratings fell by the same degree in both groups. Interestingly, by halfway through the study the TLP subjects were less satisfied with their treatment than the control patients, although by the end the two groups gave their respective treatments equal ratings for effectiveness.

"You don't always need face-to-face communication to produce behavioural change," says Sharon Dolezal, the psychologist who led the study. But she insists that such programs will never completely replace face-to-face therapy.

Cost-Effective Mental Illness

Cost-effective, automated systems of diagnosis and treatment are in demand in the US. According to Bernard Arons, director of the Federal Center for Mental Health Services in Rockville, Maryland, the American healthcare system is shifting towards preventive care, with individuals making small down payments and insurance companies shouldering more of the financial burden, in order to avoid having to pay for costly long-term health problems. As those companies expand and take on a broader spectrum of patients, their reluctance to pay for potentially long-term treatment like psychotherapy increases.

But to be truly preventive, such a mental healthcare system would need to reach more people, says Arons, particularly those who live in remote areas, who are housebound through physical disability, who are reluctant to consult their doctor, or who require specialist treatment for which they have to travel long distances. "At the moment we're looking into some sort of telemedicine hook-up where you can see each other as well as exchange information," he says.

Ross Goldstein, a psychologist at a private consultancy in San Francisco, believes that as face-to-face therapy becomes more and more of a rarity, people will look for other ways to get help. "Psychotherapy is still being practised largely in the manner it has been for the past hundred years without recognising that people's needs have changed," he says.

The popularity of self-help groups on the Internet seems to support that view. As one subscriber to MADNESS, an electronic action, information and discussion mailgroup for people who experience mood swings, panic attacks, voices and visions, explains: "I was able to talk about things I wouldn't even dare talking about to anyone who knew me. The anonymity is important to me."

E-mail counselling seems like an obvious progression. But this is where many psychotherapists draw the line. Without body language, tone of voice and everything else that comes with face-to-face communication, they argue, how can an accurate diagnosis be made? "It's not merely a question of visual and nonverbal clues, but also of the so-called 'therapeutic container'," says Steve Bond, president of a World Wide Web information service for psychological professionals called Online Psychological Services. "I think there's enough research to support saying that the human relationship, regardless of what is said or suggested, has a therapeutic effect in itself. So the question is, can an Internet relationship really be a therapeutic relationship?"

There are also ethical objections. What if either patient or therapist wants to terminate the relationship while the other does not—could they protect themselves from incoming mail? How would you ensure client confidentiality? Should therapists offering such services via the Internet be regulated, and if so how?

Out of Control

The British Psychological Society still lacks a statutory register of members, so in theory anyone in Britain can set themselves up as a psychotherapist. In the US, says Arons, psychotherapists are licensed by the state in which they practice, not by the federal government, so dissatisfied clients do have a clear route for redress. But the Internet does not recognise state boundaries so, for example, these regulations would not protect a Dutch person who decided to take advice from a Californian therapist. This could put at risk the very people who would benefit most from online therapy—people who are unwilling or unable to leave their homes, and are therefore least likely to seek a second opinion or check their therapist's credentials by other means.

Even if full-blown counselling over the Internet remains a health economist's dream, there is no doubt that some aspects of psychotherapy are moving into cyberspace. Take the American e-mail service Shrinklink, for example.

An individual can contact Shrinklink with one question of a psychological nature, which will be answered for a fee of $20. If necessary, the caller is referred to a psychologist, psychiatrist or therapist, but repeated questions are discouraged. A spokesman for Shrinklink insists that this is not therapy, and the Ethics Committee of the American Psychological Association has raised no objections.

"One of the ingredients of any kind of counselling is information," says Goldstein. "Psychologists who do not make that information available on telephone or Internet services are missing a terrific opportunity."

ELECTROCONVULSIVE THERAPY AS A LAST RESORT

Kathleen Hirsch

According to Kathleen Hirsch, electroconvulsive therapy (ECT), commonly known as shock treatment, has gained notoriety for its severe technique and potentially damaging side effects, such as long-term memory loss. However, she writes, in recent years the use of ECT in cases of severe depression has risen. For some individuals who suffer from chronic depression, she explains, traditional talk therapy and antidepressant medication are not effective and ECT seems to be the only strategy that can combat the debilitating illness. Hirsch explores the specifics of the technique and the implications of its growing use. Hirsch is the co-editor of *Mothers: Twenty Stories of Contemporary Motherhood*.

Doctor Gordon was fitting two metal plates on either side of my head. He buckled them into place with a strap that dented my forehead, and gave me a wire to bite. I shut my eyes. . . . Whee-ee-ee-ee-ee, it shrilled, through an air crackling with blue light, and with each flash a great jolt drubbed me till I thought my bones would break and the sap fly out of me like a split plant.
—Sylvia Plath, *The Bell Jar*

The nightmarish ordeal of "shock" (electroconvulsive) therapy as it was experienced by patients like Sylvia Plath in the 1950s remains, for many of us, the specter of a medical establishment itself gone mad. And media reports that electroconvulsive therapy (ECT) as a treatment for depression is on the rise are causing concern that horrific experiences like the one Plath endured will occur again—despite assurances by practitioners that ECT is a far different procedure than it was 40 years ago. Given that women are twice as prone as men to seek professional help for depression, and because anecdotal evidence suggests ECT is used on women more often than on men, ECT is clearly becoming a women's health issue: Is it as safe and effective as a growing cadre of psychiatrists insist?

Concerns about ECT are neither surprising nor inappropriate, concedes Dr. Brian Szetela, who directs ECT Services at the University of Massachusetts Medical Center in Worcester. "Back in the 1940s and

Reprinted from Kathleen Hirsch, "Shock Therapy Makes a Comeback," *Ms.*, November/December 1995, by permission of *Ms.* magazine, ©1995.

'50s, when there weren't a lot of medications specific for different psychiatric conditions, ECT was one thing that was known to be effective," he says. "There was probably a tendency to overuse it." Today, he says, we know more, both about the uses of antidepressants to control self-destructive behaviors—*and* about depression.

According to Charles Welch, a psychiatrist at Massachusetts General Hospital and an expert on depression, the illness is, broadly speaking, a spectrum of widely divergent mood disorders. At one end are so-called environmental depressions, for which there are discernible causes. Most of us, at one time or another, suffer from this type of depression. Whether or not we seek therapy, we assume, correctly, that our feelings are temporary and can be overcome with a healthy dose of reflection and empowering behavior.

The success of antidepressant drugs such as Prozac has raised people's awareness, however, that more complex depressions are biochemical in origin. Biological depressions are highly resistant to talk therapy, and tend to be hereditary. Drugs can control the general dysfunction of these deeper depressions better than long courses of psychoanalysis ever could. But there are some depths that even drugs can't reach. And it is in this most elusive terrain that ECT claims its successes.

Of the 17.5 million people in the U.S. estimated to suffer from some form of depression, about 9.2 million have episodes of recurrent, severe depression (or what is called "major depression"), according to the National Institute of Mental Health. If left untreated, people suffering from major depression run a greatly increased risk of suicide or death from neglecting to care for themselves. In these circumstances, proponents say, ECT can be a valid and lifesaving tool.

Today in the U.S., somewhere between 45,000 and 100,000 patients are receiving ECT each year. Classic candidates include the 20 percent of patients with major depression who do not respond to drug therapy. The procedure these days is quite far from the primitive techniques of the early 1950s. Then, patients were likely to receive several weekly treatments of near-lethal amounts of electricity, for as many as 100 sessions—all without benefit of anesthesia, and often without their consent. Today, the average number of treatments is 7.5, usually with no more than three sessions a week, at far lower levels of electricity. The patient is placed under general anesthesia and given a relaxant that prevents muscle convulsions during the 15-minute procedure. Electrodes placed either on top and on one side of the head or on both sides of the head conduct electricity through the brain, enough to induce a generalized seizure that lasts between 30 and 60 seconds.

While doctors still don't fully understand how ECT works, the prevailing hypothesis is that extreme depression is somehow triggered by a malfunction of the hypothalamus (which regulates appetite, curiosity, sexual desire, concentration, and sleep cycles), and that by stimulating the hypothalamus through seizure, ECT stabilizes the brain's chemistry and restores hypothalamic function. Today, ECT works primarily as a form of acute crisis intervention, proponents say; it rescues patients from ever-deepening depression or death. The normal course of treatment after ECT calls for antidepressants, talk therapy, or additional ECT to maintain a patient's improvement. Without such follow-up, 50 percent of all ECT patients relapse within six months.

Even when ECT is successful, there remains the question of side effects—the most severe of which is memory loss, but which may also include confusion and disorientation. Anti-ECT groups claim that practitioners greatly minimize the side effects, and they question the curative claims made for a practice that one foe calls "a major insult" to the brain. Among ECT's critics are former patients who say that they can't remember whole years of their lives, or who have lost the ability to function intellectually. Dianna Loper, founder of the Austin, Texas-based World Association of Electroshock Survivors, says she has suffered memory loss for the 22 years since she received ECT. In 1994, she and other Texas activists led an unsuccessful bid to make ECT illegal in the state.

ECT advocates concede that short-term memory loss does occur in most cases, but they contend that this usually resolves itself in several weeks and that the perception of long-term memory loss is actually a function of the depression, not the treatment. "The number one reason for persistent memory complaints after ECT is incomplete remission of the depression," says Mass General's Charles Welch. Supporters of ECT see the prospect of short-term memory loss as an acceptable risk, with consequences far less severe than a debilitating depression that may lead to death.

Critics also claim that there are potential ethical issues pertaining to the use of ECT—particularly for the elderly, who compose the majority of ECT patients. They say elderly people are at a higher risk of needless treatments, intended, perhaps, simply to make them more "manageable" at home or in nursing homes. John Breeding, an Austin-based psychologist and ECT opponent, contends: "The predominant recipients of ECT are women—especially elderly women. ECT acts as a social control mechanism—ageism and sexism are clearly acted out and reinforced."

Nevertheless, Dr. Ellen Frank, an expert on older women and depression, who directs the Women's Study at the Western Psychiatric Institute and Clinic in Pittsburgh, insists there is a good reason why ECT is used more frequently on the older population. "Despite its bad press, and despite the lay image of ECT as being a horrible, traumatic treatment, it actually turns out to be the safest way we have of getting someone out of major depression," she says. "All of the [antidepressant] medications we use have some risks associated with them. I know this is hard for the lay person to understand, but it's safer." She adds: "I've never, ever recommended ECT to a patient who didn't thank me in the end. Never."

But how do doctors determine who should be a candidate for ECT—is it appropriate for the millions of women who are using Prozac and other antidepressants? Many of them have symptoms that are identical to what are now described in the medical literature as the clinical indications for ECT treatment: weight loss, early morning awakening, impaired concentration, pessimistic mood, motor restlessness, and anorexia. Practitioners say it's virtually unthinkable that a doctor would recommend ECT before trying drug therapy: the American Psychiatric Association's protocol for ECT clearly directs psychiatrists to make several attempts with antidepressants before considering ECT. "If you're really unsure of what you're dealing with," in terms of what type of depression a patient is suffering from, says Welch, "then the only reasonable thing to do is embark on a regime of a good antidepressant plus the best shot you can give it at psychotherapy." Unnecessary damage is done, he adds, by psychiatrists who are too slow to use ECT on patients who haven't responded to more conventional therapies. "In my opinion, you can't treat major depression with psychotherapy any more than you can treat hypothyroidism or diabetes with psychotherapy. It's a terrible, cruel irony that there are so many clinicians who try to do so."

Nevertheless, Amy Banks, a psychiatrist at the Center for Women's Development at the Human Resources Institute in Brookline, Massachusetts, cautions women to be vigilant, and to make as informed a judgment as possible about their choice of treatments. Banks says she entered medical school as a committed feminist, convinced that she would never "resort" to ECT. Over the years, she has become a convert to ECT's effectiveness in specific situations. She has referred several patients for ECT and is convinced that it saved their lives. All the same, she advises, "Doctors need to do a very thorough risk-benefit analysis." For example, she cautions, ECT can be inappropriate for women with a history of sexual or physical abuse, as the treatment may conjure up the feelings of powerlessness first induced by the abuse. "Patients ought to explore all medical possibilities," says Banks. "Don't jump into it."

Ellen Frank advises family members to be as involved as possible in helping a patient make the decision about whether to undergo ECT. "There's no question that someone who has an incapacitating depression has a limited capacity for informed consent," she says. "Their concentration impairment is so severe that they can't remember what's being said or being told to them. Close family members should be sure that they really do understand what is going on." They should insist that the doctor explain what the procedure consists of, how it's done, what the possible side effects or adverse effects might be, and whether there are any alternative treatments. The doctor should also monitor the patient between sessions, says Brian Szetela. "Even if the patient has signed the consent form," he says, "she can reverse her decision at any point in the treatment."

Despite its renewed legitimacy, ECT remains what is known in psychological parlance as an "extraordinary treatment." In responsible hands, it is the treatment of last resort, and even then only for a small subset of the population. If it isn't a panacea, neither is it the cruel and punitive ordeal it once was.

CHAPTER 4

THE DEBATE OVER ANTIDEPRESSANTS

CHALLENGING PROZAC

Peter R. Breggin

Peter Kramer's *Listening to Prozac* strengthened the popularity of the use of antidepressants—especially Prozac—for depression. According to Peter Breggin, however, people who take Prozac often experience negative side effects, with serious consequences. In the following selection, excerpted from his book *Talking Back to Prozac*, Breggin relays horrific incidents of Prozac's effects on patients. He asserts that the harmful influence of this mood-altering drug can devastate lives far worse than depression. A psychiatrist in private practice in Bethesda, Maryland, Breggin is the founder and national director of the Center for the Study of Psychiatry and Psychology, also in Bethesda. He is the author of *Toxic Psychiatry* and *Talking Back to Ritalin*.

While many patients and professionals seem to be listening to Prozac—that is, to its manufacturer, Eli Lilly, and to the medical-industrial complex that promotes medication—a hitherto underground movement of Prozac survivors is making an increasing public impact. Guy McConnell of Clovis, California, is president of the Prozac Survivors Support Group, a national organization previously directed by Louisville, Kentucky, resident Bonnie Leitsch, who became suicidal while taking Prozac.

The members of the national Prozac Survivors Support Group include hundreds of former patients and their friends and families. Sometimes the member is a survivor of Prozac, sometimes a friend or relative of someone who became emotionally disturbed, or committed suicide or murder, while on Prozac. McConnell became involved after his fiancée, seemingly out of the blue, strangled her mother to death with a drapery cord. The fiancée was taking Prozac at the time.

The Prozac Survivors Support Group is wholly independent, receives no funding from anyone, and is not affiliated with crank groups or cults. It is run by volunteers.

The survivor group files contain hundreds of cases: The man who thought his cow was leaning to one side and tried to straighten the animal by backing a tractor into it; the woman who thought the roof of her home was dirty and became enraged when her husband didn't appreciate her sitting up there for hours to clean it by hand; ordinary folks who suddenly embezzle or rob banks, and then throw the money away on outlandish schemes.

Negative Prozac Incidents Abound

I have been working closely with the Prozac survivors, addressing their annual conventions, helping them publicize their existence, and benefiting from their moral support and the vast experience reflected in their hundreds of members. I wish more psychiatrists would ask these groups, "What is your data showing?" Our Center for the Study of Psychiatry has published a report that summarizes and evaluates the Prozac survivors' experiences.

I already knew innumerable Prozac horror stories, but I began to meet new survivors and to hear about new tragedies when I appeared on TV talk shows. On one show, a brother and sister gave their contrasting views of the drug. The sister had "crashed" and become suicidal after a few weeks of feeling energized on Prozac. More recently her brother had been prescribed Prozac for anxiety related to the Los Angeles earthquake of 1994. After a few weeks on the drug, he felt like he was living fully for the first time in his life. He felt more alert, brighter, and happier than ever; but his sister saw ominous personality changes in him, a way of being "out of touch" that mirrored the changes she herself had experienced shortly before she crashed.

On another show, another brother and sister told a far more grim story. Their father, a kind and gentle man who had never been suicidal or aggressive, took Prozac for stress and fatigue. According to his two children, under the drug's influence, without warning or provocation, he stabbed his wife—their mother—to death. After inflicting multiple wounds on her, he killed himself.

In the same week, an attorney called me with yet another sad tale—a woman physician who had prescribed Prozac for herself to combat the stress of starting up a practice and ended up shooting herself. Her husband, a surgeon, was suing Eli Lilly, the manufacturer of Prozac, for failure to warn people about the dangers of the drug. He would have to stand in line behind two dozen or more others who were filing similar suits. Then another attorney called to tell me about a man who had murdered his boss and almost killed his wife while he was taking Prozac.

The Example of Gina's Experience

Meanwhile, my own clinical experience with Prozac has confirmed the existence of the drug's dark side. As a result of my earlier books, including *Toxic Psychiatry*, and my work as director of the Center for the Study of Psychiatry, I am at times a beacon to people who have been hurt, frustrated, or humiliated by biopsychiatric treatment.

Many patients come to me after having failed to improve on a variety of medications. Often they have been damaged by earlier biopsychiatric treatments.

Suffering from chronic neck pain after a skiing accident in Colorado, Gina (names have been changed), a twenty-seven-year-old woman, had been referred to me by her orthopedist. She had been prescribed a variety of analgesics, and while they helped to relieve her pain, they tended to sap her energy. She'd also been given several different antidepressants, sometimes to ease her physical pain and at other times to treat her depression. She said, "They just didn't do much for me."

Seven years earlier, Gina had fled from her traditional Sicilian family and come to the United States as a student. She loved her mother and father very much, but chose to reject her father's authoritarian attitudes as well as her mother's and sister's subservience to the males in the family. Gina was simply too spirited—too spontaneously independent—to stand for it.

It was easy for me to believe Gina when she described how she arrived in this country as a student with only a few remote family contacts, learned English in a matter of months, and then demonstrated an unanticipated aptitude for science. She was now a research assistant at a rising biotech firm while at the same time getting her master's degree in microbiology.

My psychiatric practice continually confirms the formative influence of childhood in the lives of adults, yet I am regularly astonished at how some people manage to reach adulthood with an intensity of energy and personal courage that seems wholly unexplained in terms of their background. Gina, full of life, was one of them. Out of the bulwark of traditionalism and patriarchy came this brave, self-determined young person. Even while pacing my office in physical pain and emotional despair, Gina emanated spiritual energy.

The skiing accident had occurred eighteen months earlier, leaving Gina with pain and spasms secondary to bruising in the region of her cervical vertebrae. Gina's work in the biotech lab required focusing her eyes through microscopes and calibrating instruments, while turning her head back and forth to make notes or to draw sketches. The effort created tensions in her neck that stymied her recovery. But she resisted taking vacations, let alone sick leave, and so she fought against the pain, tried to keep working, and got worse.

The research chief in Gina's department had singled her out as a rising star and had already included her among the string of more credentialed authors on an upcoming scientific paper. She routinely put in extra hours at the lab and then additional hours going to class and studying. She couldn't let up; she didn't want to let up. She had, in her own words, a "go-go" style. Now, partially disabled by the injury, she was depressed and even suicidal for the first time in her life.

Until the accident, Gina's love life had been as exciting and seemingly ideal as her career. Six years earlier, she had met and soon married Jake, a Jewish-American art dealer. "I was hardly settled down in America," she explained, when she had strolled off the street into an art show at Jake's gallery and, across the crowded room, he'd been drawn by her vibrancy. It began with his offering her a glass of wine and quickly blossomed into a storybook romance. She had worked for a time in his gallery, and then begun school and her eventual career.

Gina described Jake as the most wonderful man imaginable—and promptly began to sob. Their romance had been perfect, or so she thought, until the last year or so. In the beginning, their friends had seen them as the ideal couple. Even her mother and father—to her surprise—overcame the shock of her relationship with a Jewish-American man. After the marriage, they had met and come to accept her warm, vibrant husband. He had capped his trip to Italy by taking them on an art tour of Rome.

Their tradition-oriented families turned out to have much in common, and Gina loved and was loved by Jake's parents. She developed a wide circle of friends, some through school, others through the gallery and work.

"Gone," she told me sadly. "They're all gone."

Turning Away from Loved Ones

Six months earlier, she had left her husband and rejected all of her friends. "I was determined," she said, "to do it on my own."

"But your husband—I've never heard a woman speak so lovingly of a man she's determined to divorce."

I don't usually challenge my clients too strongly in the first few sessions of therapy, but her story didn't make emotional sense.

"Gina," I said, "when people are so much in love and have a few years of really good married-time behind them, they don't usually quit so quickly. What was going on?"

"When I made the decision, I felt like I had 'had it with him,'" she said. Then she added, "Besides, I was feeling that way with everyone. I had had it with everyone."

"It still doesn't make sense," I persisted. "He was going through stresses and not faring too well, maybe coming apart, not being himself. And so were you. But the change in your feelings—it sounds so abrupt and final for someone so in love."

"Jake's dad is retired, and he got sick about that time," Gina started to recall the sequence of events. "So Jake went to Palm Springs to help out." It was hard for her to sort out what had happened over these difficult and trying months, and she hadn't pieced this part of the story together. "While Jake was gone—it was a couple of weeks—I got a whole new feeling about being alone. All of a sudden, I felt like I didn't need him or anyone else. I was fine all by myself. Perfect! I began fighting on the phone with my parents. And then I called Jake in California and said I wanted a separation, and he freaked out, and his mom and dad, well they got really angry, and I basically told them all to go to hell."

She stopped as if surveying her life's wreckage for the first time.

"And when my friends said, 'Gina, what are you doing?', I just told them to go to hell, too. Pretty soon, there wasn't anybody."

She stopped for a moment and said, "It doesn't make sense, does it?" Tears were running down her cheeks.

She got up, paced, and then sat back down again, pulling tissues out of the box.

"Gina," I asked, "were you taking any psychiatric medications at the time?"

"Probably."

"Which ones?"

She had to think hard to recall. "A week or two before Jake went away to San Francisco, I got started with a new doctor. He gave me . . . yes. . . . It was Prozac."

During a period of three weeks on Prozac, Gina had rejected everyone in her life.

Any person's life is far too complex to capture in a few paragraphs. Surely many factors, known and unknown, had brought Gina to drive away her friends and relations, and to teeter now on the brink of suicide. But what struck me, and Gina also, was the abruptness of her complete rejection of all the people who loved her and whom she loved as well.

Could Gina's transformation be attributed entirely to Prozac? We can never be certain of this, but starting Prozac coincided with Gina's sudden withdrawal of feeling from family and friends. Ordinarily, it might have seemed like a curiosity, something to be tucked away for future use. But I was recalling something I had already tucked away— a conversation with Ann Tracy, Utah Director of the Prozac Survivors Support Group. It was one of the first things Ann shared with me. She explained, "A lot of what we're seeing is people losing their feeling for the people in their lives. They stop caring about their husbands or wives, or their children. They stop caring about God." Ann knew first-hand. When the man she loved had started taking Prozac, he'd pulled away from her and from everyone else.

The Prozac Craze Perspective

The moral and psychological dangers posed by Prozac are ultimately more threatening than its physical side effects. But this is not the first time that America has fallen unabashedly in love with a *prescription* medication. Until the danger of addiction became obvious, Valium enjoyed an escalating reputation as "mother's little helper." Housewives throughout the country got through their humdrum, frustrating daily chores by remaining in a drug-induced fog. But Valium never benefited from medical and media claims that it improved the normal human condition. The picture is more complicated with the amphetamines, drugs that in many ways resemble Prozac. Three decades ago, very similar claims were made for their special life-enhancing properties.

While Prozac is not the first prescription drug epidemic, it has garnered a degree of media support never before encountered, as well as a best-selling book by Peter Kramer to fuel its popularity. Kramer bases his theory of Prozac-induced personality transformation on nothing more than a handful of his own cases. He shows a naïve reliance on the manufacturer of Prozac, Eli Lilly, in his discussion of the drug's impact on the brain. In particular, he shows too little awareness of the pharmacological mechanisms that could cause the opposite of Prozac's intended effect, leading patients to become violent or depressed and suicidal. He gives no credence to the Prozac survivor movement.

Kramer argues that Prozac can transform personality for the better but largely dismisses the far more likely possibility that, like any psychoactive drug, it can transform it for the worse. In passing, he makes frequent comparisons of Prozac to amphetamines and cocaine, but ends up superficially rejecting the clinical implications without fully examining the comparisons. He sprinkles his book with moral considerations, but does not seem to take them seriously. While touting the drug's capacity to reduce sensitivity to oneself and others, he fails to face the implications of creating a society of less-in-touch, less-caring, and less-loving human beings. He seems enamored with his concluding observation that "In time, I suspect we will come to discover that modern psychopharmacology has become, like [Sigmund] Freud in his day, a whole climate of opinion under which we conduct our different lives."

In my conversations with Kramer and in his media appearances, he seems genuinely concerned that his book has helped to fuel the Prozac craze. He tries, tentatively, to caution the country about moral concerns. On a talk show we appeared on together, he warned that there's no way to anticipate Prozac's potentially damaging effects on the developing brains of children and adolescents. Nevertheless, his book has misled hundreds of thousands of readers and millions more who have heard its message of better living through chemistry.

Ask Questions of Prozac

It's time to address the real issues and questions about Prozac:

- Did Prozac perform well or even adequately during the Food and Drug Administration (FDA) approval trials, or was the FDA overeager to approve it?
- What are the real adverse effects of Prozac and has the FDA told the public everything it knows?

- What is Prozac's short-term and long-term impact on the brain?
- Is Prozac a clinical and pharmacological cousin to "speed" and cocaine?
- Do some people really function better on Prozac and, if so, what does that mean about their lives?
- Can Prozac encourage or worsen someone's tendency toward violence, depression, and suicide?
- How did Prozac win FDA approval despite its potentially life-threatening behavioral side effects, and why did the agency exonerate the drug at its September 1991 hearing?
- What economic and political forces have backed the promotion of the drug?
- Why is there an avalanche of lawsuits against Eli Lilly regarding Prozac?
- What methods does Lilly use to push America to buy its pill?
- What are the moral and spiritual implications for a nation being flooded by propaganda in favor of taking drugs?
- Are there hidden human costs to taking Prozac that may haunt the individual and end up plaguing society?
- What is depression and what are an individual's alternatives to taking drugs?

America is turning a corner with vast moral, scientific, and medical implications. We may have finally adopted a "National Prescription Drug"—and with it, the idea that drugs are the answer. In less than a generation, we have rejected the motto, "Just say no to drugs," and adopted the motto, "Take this drug to improve your life." It is time for opposing voices. It's time to talk back to Prozac.

THE PROGRESS OF PROZAC

Nancy Wartik

Since 1985, the year when the Food and Drug Administration (FDA) approved the use of Prozac for depression, this antidepressant has gained both fame and notoriety, Nancy Wartik explains in the following selection. Wartik, a writer specializing in health and psychology, surveys developments in the use of Prozac as well as the drug's impact in reshaping society's view of depression. While Prozac is not effective for all those who suffer from depression, Wartik stresses, for some patients, the drug is crucial for combating the disorder.

In 1991, a traumatic sexual encounter sent Cindy Thompson (name has been changed), now 41, plummeting into depression. "It was agonizing," recalls Thompson, a public relations consultant in Baltimore. "I wanted to kill myself every day." Thompson's psychotherapist recommended Prozac. "But I resisted," she says. "I was concerned about using a chemical to alter my mind and emotions." Finally, poised between the knife drawer and the telephone, "I called my therapist." Thompson agreed to be briefly hospitalized—and to try Prozac. "I figured I'd hit bottom and had nothing left to lose."

Nineteen-ninety-six marks a decade since Prozac, the antidepressant that's achieved a celebrity normally associated with movie stars and rock groups, first hit the market. Since then, it's been glorified as a miracle cure and vilified in a backlash centering on claims that Prozac makes some users violent. It's also been attacked as a "happy pill," a quick fix that allows users to ignore the psychological issues at the root of their depression.

Yet even with its luster tarnished, Prozac prospers. With 1995 sales topping $2 billion, up 24% from 1994, it's the second biggest money-making drug in the U.S., after the ulcer medicine Zantac. According to the manufacturer, Eli Lilly, more than 14 million Americans have joined the Prozac generation.

The drug has touched the lives of women in particular, primarily because they're twice as likely as men to suffer from major depression—a partly generic disorder marked by persistent symptoms including sadness, fatigue, sleep or appetite problems and suicidal thoughts.

Reprinted from Nancy Wartik, "Prozac: The Verdict Is In," *American Health*, November 1996, with permission.

Women also tend to have higher rates of other disorders for which Prozac is now prescribed, such as dysthymia (chronic mild depression), some forms of anxiety (panic attacks and obsessive-compulsive disorder), severe PMS and bulimia.

Has the advent of Prozac been a boon for women, or will it come to be seen as the 1990s equivalent of "Mother's Little Helper"? Has the drug transformed the treatment of mental illness, or will it cause as yet unknown health problems down the line? Such questions are all the more pressing in this era of managed care, when there's a growing tendency to treat psychological disorders with medication rather than prolonged (read: pricey) talk therapy. And with a host of newer antidepressant clones such as Zoloft, Paxil and Serzone flooding the market, should Prozac still reign as the drug of choice? Ten years into the Prozac phenomenon, we're starting to get some answers.

A Revolution in Treatment

Antidepressants work by altering balances of mood-regulating chemicals, such as serotonin in the brain. The most popular antidepressants used to be a class of drug known as tricyclics, which were developed in the 1950s and are still in use. But tricyclics affect not only the brain chemicals they're supposed to but also some they aren't. This can lead to side effects ranging from constipation, dizziness and weight gain to more dangerous problems such as heart rhythm abnormalities.

In contrast, Prozac, Paxil and Zoloft, which belong to a class of drugs known as selective serotonin reuptake inhibitors, or SSRI's, affect serotonin regulation much more directly, which means users tolerate them better. "It doesn't matter how well a drug works if, because of the side effects, people don't take it regularly," says Michael Norden, M.D., a psychiatrist at the University of Washington in Seattle and author of *Beyond Prozac*. "So Prozac was a tremendous step forward."

Women in particular seem to find Prozac and the other SSRI's easy to tolerate. In a multicenter study of people with chronic depression, women and men were randomly assigned to tricyclic or SSRI treatment. More than 25% of the women on tricyclics stopped taking them, largely because of the side effects, while less than 15% of women on SSRI's quit. They also reported better moods while using SSRI's. (Men, on the other hand, tended to do better on tricyclics.)

With findings such as these, it comes as no surprise that antidepressants are now prescribed more liberally than ever. Some 60% are given out by family doctors, rather than mental health specialists. They're also prescribed for a far greater range of ailments and for less serious disorders: Whereas tricyclics were once reserved only for those with severe depression, these days it's not uncommon for physicians to prescribe Prozac for a case of the blues.

Prozac's easy accessibility has also raised fears that doctors are handing out the drug like M&M's and people are popping it for "personality face-lifts." The real story is more complicated. Plenty of experts agree that the drugs are too readily available. "Their popularity has led to some inappropriate use," says Sidney Zisook, M.D., a professor of psychiatry at the University of California at San Diego. "There are a lot of sloppy diagnoses, cases where they're given for the wrong reasons or for too long. There are also patients who just want to be perfect, to always enjoy themselves, and they think they can do it the easy way, with Prozac. But it's wrong to use these medicines to try to solve all of life's problems."

Others point to a tendency, encouraged by managed care, for doctors to prescribe a pill instead of steering patients toward psychotherapy. "There are maybe 20% to 30% of depressed patients who can just take a drug and get well," says New York University psychiatrist Eric Peselow, M.D. "But the majority need psychotherapy as part of treatment. Racing to Prozac isn't the only answer." Unfortunately people who pop a pill without doing the hard work of self-examination may find themselves back where they started when they quit taking the medication.

Yet with only one in three depressed people today getting treatment, cries of "Prozac abuse!" can be misleading. "There are far more people who could benefit from these drugs and aren't taking them than there are people taking them inappropriately," says Dr. Zisook. Prozac's trendiness shouldn't obscure the fact that the drug and its progeny help many people dramatically.

Despite her initial skepticism, for instance, Thompson found the drug "life transforming. I felt like myself again." Prozac also pulled Isabel Leigh (name has been changed) up from despair. Leigh, 41, a New York City editor who has struggled with depression on and off for years, was reluctant to try the drug. "I didn't want to be just one more trendy Prozac taker," she says. "I told myself it was a crutch I could do without." But in 1995 she found herself feeling lethargic, hopeless and unable to concentrate; she withdrew from friends and let work slide. Finally Leigh went to a doctor and got a Prozac prescription. "It took a few weeks, but the difference was incredible," she says. "I realized I'd been trying to overcome a biochemical problem with willpower alone."

Prozac Pitfalls

Glowing testimonials aside, Prozac isn't perfect. Like any currently available antidepressant, it works in only 60% to 70% of cases. There's often a lag of up to eight weeks before the drug starts working. And Prozac isn't free of side effects either: Potential problems include agitation, insomnia, headache and weight gain or loss. What's more, perhaps a third of those who stay on Prozac for nine months or more find that its uplifting effects fade away, a problem ingloriously known as "Prozac poopout." (Increasing the dose once or twice often helps.)

A growing number of studies also show that up to half of all Prozac users experience decreased libido and delayed or no orgasm. Sharon Keene (name has been changed), 39, a writer in Laguna Hills, CA, took Prozac for three months and "it seemed to help in just about every way," she says. "But I ended up stopping, because I couldn't achieve orgasm. If I wasn't married, maybe I wouldn't have cared so much, but it was affecting my relationship with my husband."

Though other SSRI's can impair sexual function too, Zoloft and Paxil leave the bloodstream faster than Prozac, so users may be able to circumvent trouble in bed by taking drug "holidays" a day or two before the act (so much for spontaneity). Serzone, on the market since 1995, is kinder to users' sex lives. So is Wellbutrin, a medication with a slightly different mechanism of action than Serzone and the SSRI's. It does add a very slight risk of seizures, though.

The bottom line: None of the new antidepressants is clearly superior. "They all have advantages and disadvantages," says Dr. Zisook. "We never know with certainty which drug will work best. There's always some trial and error involved."

The Price of Fame

As the leader of the pack, Prozac is often the drug of choice by benefit of name recognition alone. But its fame works against it too. Even today Prozac's reputation is clouded by rumors it can't quite shake. Within two years of its introduction in the U.S., headlines and lawsuits began claiming that Prozac drives some users to bizarre, violent behavior. One notorious 1989 incident, the subject of a book called *The Power to Harm* by John Cornwell, involved a 47-year-old printing plant worker who shot 20 coworkers and then committed suicide after being on Prozac. Survivors and relatives of the victims sued Eli Lilly and lost, but the damage to Prozac's reputation was done.

Today you can surf the Net and still find horror stories from disgruntled folks in "Prozac survivor" support groups. Mary Beth Mrozek, a 33-year-old Buffalo, NY, mother of three who has bipolar illness, says that while on the drug she hallucinated, became convinced people were plotting against her and violently attacked loved ones. "I was a totally different person," she says.

Should the average Prozac user worry about having a Jekyll and Hyde reaction? Bipolar patients who take Prozac may be at slightly higher risk for an episode of mania. But that's a risk associated with any antidepressant (though possibly less so with Wellbutrin). Based on a substantial body of research, experts agree that Prozac users overall aren't at greater risk for violent or suicidal behavior. In fact, says Dr. Norden, "Depressed people who avoid Prozac are probably placing themselves in greater danger. Nothing increases suicide risk as much as depression itself."

A Cancer Connection?

Perhaps a more realistic worry involves unknowns about the long-term effects of Prozac and the other SSRI's, especially since some users are now staying on the drugs indefinitely. A slender body of evidence, based mostly on animal and very preliminary human studies, suggests that antidepressants, including Prozac, could accelerate tumor growth in some people who have a predisposition to cancer or preexisting tumors. Not surprisingly, Eli Lilly disputes these findings. "Lilly's long-term animal studies have been extensively reviewed by the FDA," says Freda Lewis-Hall, M.D., a psychiatrist who heads the Lilly Center for Women's Health in Indianapolis. "There is absolutely no scientifically credible evidence that it either causes or promotes cancer."

Not everyone agrees. Oncologist Lorne Brandes, M.D., of the Manitoba Cancer Treatment and Research Foundation in Winnipeg, Canada, questions how carefully Lilly interpreted some of its data. But at the same time, he says that antidepressants are "absolutely warranted to treat depression. I'd just suggest trying to get off them as soon as you comfortably can."

Ultimately, however, we may remember Prozac not for its side effects, trendiness or even its effectiveness, but for the attention it has focused on depression—and that can only benefit women in the end. "Once, to be depressed was to be morally and spiritually weak," says Dr. Zisook. "Now people in line at the grocery store are talking about being on Prozac. The drug has brought depression out of the closet."

Leigh, for one, is grateful that it did. "It's not like I have a perfect life with Prozac," she says. "I still have ups and downs. But now I know that if I do get down, I'll come back up. Before Prozac, I was never sure."

DEPRESSED PATIENTS NEED MORE THAN DRUGS

Deborah Franklin

Prozac and other antidepressants work by boosting the brain's level of serotonin, a neurotransmitter or chemical "messenger" between cells that greatly affects mood. However, asserts Deborah Franklin, a staff writer for *Health*, nondrug alternatives can also cause serotonin levels to rise. Talk therapy, she maintains, has been proven to have the ability to raise mood-boosting chemicals in the brain and has been effective in treating depression. According to Franklin, the attention that Prozac has received and the frequent prescription of the drug to treat depression has over-shadowed talk therapy's success in providing depressed patients with lasting treatment. Although medication may help depressed patients, Franklin contends, talk therapy is an integral part of recovery and should not be neglected.

For 21 years they have sought him out, three or four people every day, each unhappy in his or her own way. There are chain-smoking sales-men too hostile to sit, sunken-eyed students unable to sleep, widows whose lips tremble, eyes brim at the mere mention of a husband three years dead. Whatever the heart-numbing loss, and perhaps especially when the agitation or fog seems to arise from no loss at all, they are referred to Victor I. Reus or others like him—neuroscientists, the lead-ing emotional healers of our clay.

Reus is a psychiatrist and professor of psychopharmacology at the University of California at San Francisco and, as such, tends to be a wizard of last resort. He is a counselor's counselor—the guy the pastor or family doctor sends you to when getting more exercise, easing back at the office, or leaning on friends isn't enough. As a medical doctor, the only brand of psychological healer in the United States permitted to prescribe drugs, he mostly gets patients looking for exactly that. And thanks to a recent boom in transformative pills to ease depres-sion, Reus quite often does have something chemical to offer.

But lately he has noticed that many patients come to him not just depressed, but confused.

Reprinted from Deborah Franklin, "Treat Depression with More Than Drugs," *Health*, April 1997, by permission of *Health*, ©1997.

"I hear it again and again," Reus says. "They'll sit down and say, 'Look, I've been to other docs who tell me my problem comes from a chemical imbalance in my brain, and they want to give me a drug. But no one has ever actually *tested* me for an imbalance, and that is where I want you to start.'"

At which point Reus has to break it to the peeved patient as gently as he can: "I could spend a lot of your money taking pictures of your brain, and chances are there will be nothing wrong with it that we can peg your symptoms to," he tells them. "I can measure levels of serotonin in your blood or cerebral spinal fluid, and still that won't tell me anything useful. After all that testing, I'll be in the same position as every other doctor: I can recommend psychotherapy and one or another drug that has helped other people with your symptoms, and then we'll just have to watch and see how you do."

Really? The news, Reus says, always comes as a bit of a shock. This is the Decade of the Brain, for Freud's sake, and faith in biological precision is riding high. "Getting inside someone's head" these days is less often about analyzing thoughts and feelings than snapping pictures of them with the help of PET scans that illustrate in brilliant color the parts of the brain that rev up or shut down during a funk, and MRIs that offer up photographic slices of gray matter without ever cracking a skull. Besides serotonin, researchers have identified more than 60 other chemical messengers, or neurotransmitters, up from just a handful a few decades ago. Today it is undisputed that severe mental illness is rooted in a chemical mix-up of some sort—whether prompted by an inborn miswiring of the brain or by a virus, environmental toxin, or psychological trauma that has somehow knocked a person's brain chemistry out of whack. "Good-bye Oedipus," an article in a recent issue of *Time* magazine declared. "The three-pound organ that rules the body is finally giving up its secrets."

Depression, once seen exclusively as a stumble of the spirit, has been recast in the popular imagination as just another physical imbalance, like diabetes or iron-poor blood. "My wife has depression," General Colin Powell mentioned at a press conference in 1995. "It is not a family secret. It is very easily controlled with proper medication, just as my blood pressure is." *Next question?*

The Cold, Hard Truth

That's fine, of course. Surely any drug that safely enables even a fraction of those suffering from depression or other mood disorders to resume full lives should be celebrated. When a life has been wrenched to a standstill by pain—whether by the shrill torment of daily migraines or the deeper growl of fierce depression—the immediate goal is to make it stop.

But trouble begins when, like a garbled message in the party game telephone, word comes down that the chemical imbalance underlying depression is simply a serotonin deficiency, with Prozac and other serotonin-boosters the obvious cure. The cold, hard truth is that even when these drugs work, no one really knows how or why.

That single, widespread misconception—that the new drugs cure depression the same way vitamin D prevents rickets, or vitamin C fixes scurvy—feeds a host of all-too-practical problems, ranging from the discounting of a drug's serious side effects to the assumption that what's needed is a lifelong prescription. Saddest of all, the misplaced faith may lead us to spurn treatments that work just as well—or even better.

Prozac's Monopoly

Of all the developments that have primed Americans to think of lasting anguish as a simple chemical deficiency, none has been as seductive or pervasive as Prozac. Since the drug was introduced in 1987, the global market for it and other selective serotonin-reuptake inhibitors (SSRIs)—including Zoloft and Paxil—has mushroomed to around $4 billion. Between 1995 and 1997 alone, the number of prescriptions for these drugs has jumped by 20 percent, and the list of ailments for which they are often prescribed has stretched to include anxiety, bulimia, obsessive-compulsive disorder, premenstrual syndrome, and obesity. Eighteen million Americans—about one in every eight adults— has at one time or another been put on Prozac, out of 24 million people worldwide. And today it's not the psychiatrist but the family doctor who writes far and away the most prescriptions. These generalists, who tended to shy away from the older antidepressants, have been much freer with the SSRIs because they require fewer daily doses, less monitoring, and seem to have a higher margin of safety.

The theory behind these drugs has been repeated ad infinitum: Prozac is said to lift spirits by boosting the brain's stores of serotonin, a ringleader among the chemical messengers that communicate emotion and other information from cell to cell. That idea is based on computer modeling and animal studies showing that all SSRIS slow the process by which serotonin is vacuumed up from the tiny clefts between brain cells. If serotonin is allowed to linger, pooling between the cells, the feel-good message passed along is presumably stronger than it would have been without the drug.

Serotonin Sabotage

But just because Prozac both boosts serotonin and makes some depressed people feel better doesn't mean too little serotonin caused their depression, any more than headaches are brought on by an aspirin deficiency. Any neuroscientist, if pressed, will agree that the mechanisms of depression are much more complicated than a simple flick of the serotonin switch. "This myth that you can isolate and treat depression with some sort of medical version of a surgical strike, we now know, is totally bogus," says Reus.

For one thing, SSRIs help only about two-thirds of depressed patients. That's the same success rate as (or even slightly lower than) the older antidepressants—the so-called tricyclics and MAO inhibitors—which differ chemically from SSRIs and seem to interact with a much broader sampling of the brain's chemical messengers. And even when SSRIs are effective, there is generally a several-week time lag between the moment the first dose is swallowed and the point at which the drug begins to take effect. If a simple increase in serotonin directly eased depression, researchers agree, patients would start feeling better within a matter of hours or days, not weeks.

Further muddying the waters, a little-known drug from Europe called tianeptine takes the opposite tack from Prozac—it *depletes* pools of serotonin from between the same cells—and yet is quite an effective antidepressant.

Stop Listening to Prozac

Nor is any serotonin-enhancer likely to radically change you or society—despite what you may have heard. In his 1993 best-seller, *Listening to Prozac*, Rhode Island psychiatrist Peter Kramer startled and captivated readers with his reports of the way SSRIs seemed to transform his patients' personalities. Highly sensitive patients taking Prozac became more resilient, he reported, and rigid folks became more flexible. Prozac is to the shy personality, he warned, what silicone breast implants are to flat-chested models and anabolic steroids are to Olympic swimmers—a form of cosmetic, chemical enhancement that shifts the definition of acceptable and normal.

"In the science-fiction horror-story version of the interplay of drug and culture," Kramer fretted, "a boss says, 'Why such a long face? Can't you take a MoodStim before work?'"

Kramer's concern now seems a bit overlathered. For starters, ten years of experience have shown that the drugs' side effects—most notably nausea, sometimes-severe sleep disturbances, and in up to 50 percent of patients impotence, decreased libido, or an inability to reach orgasm—are significant enough that most people won't stay on the pills if their only goal is to feel less inhibited. And the drugs probably are no more transformative than the antidepressants available decades ago, Reus says. In the first documented study of SSRI use in healthy, nondepressed people, he and colleagues at UCSF recently found that Paxil did produce some increase in self-confidence and assertiveness while decreasing negativity. "But the effects were fairly small," he says. "The drug certainly did not make anyone euphoric."

A Change in Attitude

Why are we all so eager to see depression and maybe even shyness as serotonin deficiencies—as simple, physical problems best fixed with a pill? Maybe to get around the stigmas that have long cloaked both mental illness and mood-enhancing drugs. Robert Fancher, a New York psychotherapist, argues convincingly that we Americans, born of Puritanism, have always had a difficult time owning up to our equally strong hedonistic streak. Especially today, in the just-say-no era, reaching for a drug involving the mind—even to relieve psychic pain—carries substantial shame for some people. "That sounds too much like avoiding one's problems through drugs," says Fancher, author of *Cultures of Healing: Correcting the Image of American Mental Health Care*.

But if a drug can be pitched differently, he says, not as an escape or a psychological fix, but rather as a medicine that specifically corrects a biological flaw, the stigma magically evaporates. Insulin for diabetes, iron for anemia, serotonin for distress or shyness. . . . Ah yes, we see.

It's not that neuroscientists or family doctors set out to deceive, Fancher says. Their enthusiasm for everything that modern biology *has* revealed about the brain in the last 50 years encourages them to play along, smoothing the gaps in knowledge with provisional explanations the public rushes to take up as gospel.

Chemistry Is Not Just About Drugs

Lost in the hoopla is this: Just as a drug can influence the mind's chemistry, so too can every epiphany or insight prompted by a treatment that would seem, at first blush, to have little to do with brain chemistry. In a 1996 study of people diagnosed with another psychiatric condition—obsessive-compulsive disorder—psychiatrist Jeffrey Schwartz of the University of California at Los Angeles published brightly colored PET scans taken of the patients' brains before and after each had undergone treatment with either Prozac *or* talk therapy. The results clearly showed that the treatments not only worked equally well but produced identical changes in brain metabolism. He's now beginning similar studies of depressed patients.

Given what we're learning about how different emotions reflect and influence brain activity, Schwartz's finding makes perfect sense: If you change someone's outlook, you change their brain chemistry, too. The results of a number of recent large studies of talk therapy bear this out. The very human encounter between a depressed person and a counselor trained in any of the main schools of psychotherapy has been shown to have *essentially the same success rate as medication*— around 60 or 70 percent. People who don't get relief from one or another drug are often helped by counseling, and vice versa.

Talk Therapy Is Downplayed

Yet, despite its proven effectiveness, talk therapy is being pushed toward oblivion. Already, health maintenance organizations (HMOs) and traditional insurers are chary of reimbursing patients for more than a few psychotherapy sessions. If the doctor serving as gatekeeper to further medical care can just prescribe Prozac with the stroke of a pen, the labor cost of lengthy psychotherapy can be eliminated. Simplifying the definition of depression to "serotonin deficiency" makes it easier for HMOs and family doctors to rationalize the approach. But that doesn't make it right.

"When a depressed person comes to us," Fancher says, "we don't know right away whether it's an illness itself, a sign of an illness, or a sign that the person needs to change something in his or her life." Talk therapy can help the patient discern between those sources of discomfort in a way that a 15-minute office visit and prescription for drugs can't.

"It's like if you came in with a pain in your foot," Fancher says. "You might have the pain because of a rock in your shoe or because your shoe is two sizes too small. We can give you a drug that will make you not mind the fact that your foot hurts, but wouldn't it be better to change your shoe?"

Drugs have a proper place in treatment, Fancher and most other therapists readily agree. "When depression has made somebody nonfunctional—they're missing work, say, or can't come within spitting distance of keeping up with their lives," he says, "I think you need to medicate quickly. Talking things through can only help if a patient feels well enough to talk." And even people with milder distress may find a short course of the drugs genuinely helpful.

But, Fancher says, anyone who clings to a Prozac prescription as proof that he or she is chemically deficient without the drug is making a Faustian trade. "The loss of autonomy may be the biggest risk of all," Fancher says. "If you perceive that your problem arises from a defective brain, you may start to panic if you go on vacation and your prescription runs out." Also, defining distress as a deficiency and Prozac as the cure, he says, may provide a misplaced shield for those of us whose depression arises partly from rifts in relationships or our own skewed behavior—aspects of our lives we'd do better to consciously address and try to change.

Fancher offers in illustration a male client in his late thirties whose talent, charm, and good looks had bought him years of indulgence from family and friends, despite a continuing failure to stick with a job, pay rent, or honor other adult commitments. Eventually even his nearest and dearest got tired of bailing him out, Fancher says, and as the man gradually found himself alone, he was—as you might imagine—depressed.

"He came to me for psychotherapy, and we were making some progress, but he'd heard a lot about Prozac and wanted to try it," Fancher says. "A month after he started taking the drug—about how long it takes to kick in—he decided he was fine and didn't need therapy anymore. Now he's close to 40, still can't hang on to a job, doesn't have a steady place to live, but he feels great."

CAN ANTIDEPRESSANTS INHIBIT SPIRITUAL GROWTH?

Barbara Graham

According to Barbara Graham, the prevalent use of Prozac and other antidepressants poses difficult questions for those who practice meditation and other forms of spiritual growth. In the following selection, Graham explores whether or not the personality changes caused by these medications interfere with spiritual journeys and enlightenment. For some, she writes, antidepressants provide the ability to maintain the quest for personal evolvement. For others, however, a nonmedicated approach to spiritual practice is essential for self-understanding and must include experiencing pain that antidepressants could temporarily remedy, she asserts. Graham is a playwright, a journalist, and the author of *Women Who Run with the Poodles: Myths and Tips for Honoring Your Mood Swings*.

Not long ago I plopped down on the soft upholstered chair reserved for patients in my therapist's office and jokingly announced that I thought I should try Prozac. The comment was occasioned by my reaction to psychiatrist Peter Kramer's bestselling book, *Listening to Prozac*, which I read as part of my research for this article. In chapter after chapter I had been stunned to discover how many of Kramer's stressed-out, highly sensitive patients whose lives had been transformed by Prozac *sounded a lot like me.*

What's more, it seemed as though every third person and her grandmother were on Prozac, too—proof perhaps that Aldous Huxley's *Brave New World* had arrived. I wondered: Can so many millions really be suffering from a depressive illness, or are the masses being drugged unnecessarily? After all, people like me, who function at a high level despite bouts of low self-esteem, anxiety, sadness, and an inability to always enjoy our successes, aren't *depressed;* we're garden-variety miserable. Who isn't—at least some of the time? Besides, didn't Freud tell us that the best we can hope for is ordinary misery? *Really* depressed people can't even get out of bed in the morning, I reasoned. All this obsession with Prozac struck me as just one more

Excerpted from Barbara Graham, "Meditating on Prozac," *Health*, September/ October 1994, by permission of *Health*, ©1994.

attempt by our quick-fix culture to turn complex individuals into a herd of artificially sweetened sheep.

I sat there waiting for my therapist to laugh at my suggestion: "You? Prozac? Gimme a break!" Instead he looked me squarely in the eye and said, "I think that's a really good idea." Then he whipped out his prescription pad and started writing.

Now, this is not a man who dispenses brain-altering substances lightly. In addition to being a psychiatrist with a considerable knowledge of psychopharmacology, he's a long-time Buddhist practitioner with enormous respect for the dark nights of the soul that inevitably arise during periods of intense psychological growth and spiritual practice. And he knows me well: In our three years together, the work has been profound, moving, life-changing for me and rewarding for both of us. The subject of antidepressants had come up once before, in connection with my ongoing struggle with migraines, but because I'm phobic about drugs, I declined and he didn't push it.

So when he leaned over and handed me the little piece of white paper with the word "Prozac" on it, I was speechless. Minutes passed in silence. Then it was as if all the depressed feelings that I normally defend against rose like the waters in a flash flood and overtook me. Afterward, my suffering—the lifelong pain that in some central way has defined me to myself—seemed less exquisite, less unique, less a sign of my soulfulness and depth than a possible *illness*. I felt crushed and confused.

Inundated by Prozac

With all the media attention that Prozac has attracted recently, it seems that I'm not alone in wondering whether I'm a candidate for treatment. "Since my book was published, I haven't set foot in one TV studio or newspaper office without somebody asking me if they should go on Prozac," says Kramer.

Adds New York City psychotherapist and Buddhist practitioner Diane Shainberg: "Everyone I know has considered taking it. People today want to try it the way we tried cigarettes as adolescents."

The lure is powerful: a reportedly high success rate with relatively minimal side effects, at least in the short run. (The drug hasn't been around long enough for anyone to know what the long-term effects are.) And unlike older antidepressants, Prozac and its molecular cousins Paxil and Zoloft are proving especially effective in alleviating dysthymia, a low-level form of depression that can either be chronic or occur in episodes that are briefer, less severe, and less physically disruptive than major depression. In other words, just the kind of chronic low-level depression that my therapist suggests has been affecting me on and off since childhood.

Few would argue against using antidepressants to treat severe clinical depression, but where does Prozac fever leave the rest of us? What about meditators and other introspective seekers on a spiritual path? How do we know whether we're experiencing a dark night of the soul, ordinary misery, or symptoms of a depressive illness? . . .

"Antidepressants used to be compared to aspirin," explains Klein. "Aspirin doesn't do anything unless you have a fever or an inflammation." Now a better analogy for antidepressants seems to be amphetamines. "You can give anybody an amphetamine and they'll feel less fatigued and more alert," he says. It may be that serotonin-enhancing drugs have the potential to make practically everybody have a brighter outlook.

This line of reasoning is largely responsible for fueling the current debate over the morality of prescribing a medication that might make those who are not clinically depressed feel better. For example, raising serotonin levels seems to enhance qualities such as security, courage, assertiveness, self-worth, calm, flexibility, and resilience, reports Kramer. "As soon as you say that only mental illness responds to Prozac, you're labeling as mentally ill enormous groups of people who ought not to be categorized that way," he says. Today, in addition to depression and obsessive-compulsive disorder—the only other diagnosis for which Prozac has been formally approved—serotonin boosters are being used to treat bulimia, premenstrual syndrome (PMS), impulsive aggression, anxiety, rejection sensitivity, shyness, and low self-esteem.

Who or What is Adapting?

"Really what you're doing is moving a person from one normal personality state, the melancholic temperament—a state that is uncomfortable, not particularly socially rewarded today—to another personality state that's much more rewarded," Kramer said in an interview on *Good Morning America*. Which brings us back to the question of Huxley's *Brave New World:* Instead of doing what's necessary to heal a sick society, are we medicating its members so that they can better adapt to the sickness?

"I see people who get medicated because they don't want to change what they're doing," says Shainberg. "In this fast-moving culture, people don't want to look at how they create their own unhappiness."

But, counters Mark Epstein, a New York City psychiatrist, "part of the mythology of Prozac is that it's a happy pill. In my experience, this just isn't the case. The best it can do is return you to ordinary misery and help you cope successfully with life's inevitable pain and disappointment. As a general rule, people don't respond well to antidepressants unless they need them."

The Reaction in Spiritual Circles

While Prozac may be sweeping the nation—as evidenced by the photograph of the little green-and-white capsule that appeared on the cover of *Newsweek,* not to mention the $1.2 billion in 1993 sales and the nearly 1 million prescriptions written each month—in spiritual and personal-growth circles the bias is decidedly against taking medication to feel better, often to the detriment of those who really need it.

Antonio Wood, a psychiatrist in Boulder, Colorado, and a long-time practitioner of Tibetan Buddhism, says, "Buddhists are more opinionated and puritanical than other people. They tend to think that if they work with their minds they shouldn't get depressed, which is just as ignorant as saying that if you control your thoughts you won't get cancer. People in this culture feel that if we don't do everything all by ourselves, it doesn't count."

What's more, says Wood, if anything, antidepressants are under-prescribed in circles where people tend to view their problem as a spiritual emergency—a state that definitely has more cachet than depression. "But Prozac does absolutely nothing for a dark night of the soul, which is an existential predicament," he adds.

Telling the Difference

So how do you tell the difference?

Obviously, an evaluation by a skilled clinician who is both knowledgeable about depression and attuned to the spiritual crises that may arise during meditation and other practices is critical. (Given my experience as a meditator, as well as the rigorous nature of Buddhist awareness and concentration practices, I interviewed many teachers, therapists, and patients whose primary spiritual orientation is Buddhism.) Fortunately, the difference between a dark night and a depressive episode is usually pretty clear.

"In my experience, during the course of practice, insights seldom arise in a smooth and gentle way," says Marin County, California, psychotherapist and vipassana teacher Sylvia Boorstein. "They're cataclysmic upheavals. It's like going out on a limb and sawing it off from the tree side. Suddenly you're in new territory and everything seems strange."

But, she adds, even though dark nights may include a sense of despair, they also have a vitality about them. They're compelling, not languid. The mind is awake. Depression, on the other hand, is more than an occasional episode of depressed mood; it's generally characterized by torpor and hopelessness as well as the disruption of appetite, sleep, concentration, and the capacity to experience pleasure. "To be an effective meditator, you have to have enough mind energy to practice with clarity," Boorstein explains. "When we talk about torpor as a hindrance, we may sometimes really be talking about depression."

Meditating on Prozac

One concern that depressed meditators have is that medication will distort their thinking. But, says Roger Walsh, a meditation teacher and a professor of psychiatry at the University of California, Irvine, "anti depressants may distort your cognitive processes and perceptions in some way that we don't yet understand, but I'm willing to bet the drugs cause a lot less distortion than depression does."

Robert (name has been changed), an English professor and a Zen student who suffered from chronic depression, agrees. "I kept practicing and practicing," he recalls, "but nothing was changing. I felt like I was swimming upstream against the river and constantly being thrown back, without ever making any progress. My whole outlook was pessimistic. Therapy wasn't helping. I felt trapped in my career." When a friend suggested that something biochemical might be going on, Robert—like many people on a spiritual path—resisted the idea of medication. "Just the idea of it made me feel ashamed and powerless."

Robert's reaction is fairly typical among spiritual seekers. Says Mark Epstein, a long-time meditator as well as a psychiatrist: "It's humbling to find out how much really is not under your control. It's very hard for people to adjust to that idea."

With his therapist's support, Robert was eventually evaluated by a psychopharmacologist. A lengthy questionnaire and interview confirmed that he was indeed depressed, and Prozac was prescribed. "Within days I started feeling better," he says. "The difference was striking. Suddenly the river was calm and peaceful and I started making progress. I got a new job. I became more productive and creative in my own writing. It was as if all the work I had done on the cushion finally came to fruition."

That was in 1991. Robert continues taking Prozac and has no plans to stop. As for the drug's effect on his Zen practice, he puts it this way: "There's a much more intense stillness in my practice now. And I don't beat myself up for not being a better practitioner. There's more of a sense of things being okay just as they are."

Sometimes depression is so severe that it becomes impossible to practice at all. That's what happened to Natalie (name has been changed), a Zen student and architect. In Natalie's case, it was her predisposition to depression that got her sitting *zazen* in the first place. "The Bodhisattva's vow spoke to me the first time I ever heard it," she says. "I considered my depression and the feelings that accompanied it a gift, the merciful avatar that had come to liberate me from cycles of conditioning. For years I was able to work with the depression by staying with my thoughts about it, as well as my bodily sensations, which is my practice. I could see that it was transitory, not on an intellectual level but in a very *real* way. Sitting with it allowed me not just to get out of the depression but to *be* the depression, and in being the depression, paradoxically, it shifted."

But when Natalie's marriage suddenly dissolved, she sank into a black hole of despair and was unable to stay on the cushion. "I was stunned and frightened because I had been sitting for 15 years," she recalls. An antidepressant, which she took for three months, helped her back onto the cushion. "Taking the medication was in the realm of wisdom," she says.

"But," she cautions, "just because I stopped taking it doesn't make me a better Zen student. It wasn't as if I wanted to get off the medication so that I could get back to the real thing. It's all the real thing. That's where a lot of people get confused and think they're cheating. Most of us have an internal saboteur that says, 'I've failed. If I was a *really* good Zen student, then I'd be able to use my inner resources.' I just stayed with that feeling and practiced with it. Every moment is the practice—whether you're on medication or not."

John Daido Loori, abbot of Zen Mountain Monastery in Mt. Tremper, New York, looks at it this way: "Taking medication is kind of like sitting in a chair rather than sitting cross-legged on the mat. Whether there's something wrong with people's legs or the neurotransmitters in their brain, we need to adjust the practice so that they can experience it."

Disrupting the Practice

For some depressed people, however, sitting practice without treatment actually makes them worse. "When I see Buddhist practitioners who are depressed, I recommend that they don't sit for a while," says Antonio Wood, noting that sensory deprivation tends to increase symptoms in people who are disconnected from their senses and too much in their heads to begin with.

But Prozac doesn't help everyone get back on the *zafu*. During a major life transition, Joanna (name has been changed), a sociologist and a student of Tibetan Buddhism, became severely depressed. "I thought I knew what depression was before," she recalls, "but I really had no idea. It was like being trapped inside a barren granite block I couldn't practice at all."

A psychiatrist prescribed Prozac. But instead of helping her move out of her depressed state and see things more clearly, the drug made Joanna feel even more disconnected. "It was scary," she says. "I was in a complete fog, a fuzzy, out-of-focus, cotton world. It was as if I'd been cognitively blown apart and didn't know where I was. Practice was irrelevant. I forgot that I even had one." Joanna discontinued taking the medication and set off on a long journey through Mexico, during which her depression lifted. Subsequent treatment with another antidepressant proved helpful, and she says at some point she'd like to give Prozac another try.

Getting to a Comfortable Self

Then there are those—Buddhist meditators and others—for whom Prozac is effective but who stop taking it after a short time because, unlike many people who report feeling more like themselves on the drug, they're uncomfortable with their transformed selves, even though they may feel better. "Most people I see who take Prozac are in a sort of buzz state," says Diane Shainberg. "They can do more and get more, but at the same time they don't feel like themselves."

That was the experience of Elaine (name has been changed), a painter with an interest in spirituality, who was helped enormously by Prozac in the beginning. "I felt less beaten down by life, less distraught, and less shy. Everything started to go more smoothly," she recalls. But after six months on the medication, she began to feel dull and decided to discontinue it—against her psychiatrist's advice. "When I first went off it, I felt very depressed again, but I was in the middle of moving and I was lonely; feeling depressed seemed appropriate." She adds, "Even though I'm more like I used to be, Prozac gave me a good field of comparison. Now I know what it feels like to be more trusting and carefree, so I can use that to help me through difficult times."

Which, after all, is supposed to be the point of Prozac: to give people who struggle with depression a break and an experience of what it feels like to be more comfortable with themselves and their lives—an experience, suggests Peter Kramer, where drugs do not cure but liberate people for a time so that they can progress in their exploration and understanding of themselves. "While on the medication, people make a lot of positive changes, in their sense of self, their jobs, their relationships, so that when they stop taking it they have a much bigger area of safety that will help protect them against recurrences," he says.

Although not everyone I spoke to was equally enthusiastic about the use of antidepressants, no one suggested that medication should replace psychotherapy. But with health-care reform on the national agenda, it *is* a growing concern. Says Kramer: "The big danger with managed care is that medication will take over." But, he points out, citing a University of California at Los Angeles study that looked at various treatment options and determined that a combination of medication and psychotherapy was the most effective: "The idea that we can save money by just giving medication has already been proven false before we undertake the experiment."

Prozac Does Not Always Solve the Problem

Regardless of whether somebody gets jump start out of painful, depressed feelings or is helped out of a major depression by taking medication, antidepressants are not the ultimate answer to the human predicament. For one thing, they don't work for everyone: The success rate for all classes of antidepressants ranges from 60 to 80 percent. For another, not everyone can tolerate the side effects, which in the case of Prozac can include jitteriness, insomnia, nausea, suppressed appetite, decreased libido, and delayed—or nonexistent—

orgasm. What's more, because the long-term effects are unknown, psychiatrists generally try to avoid keeping patients on them indefinitely. Then there are some people, like Elaine, who might benefit but simply don't want to take them. . . .

According to Peter Breggin, a psychiatrist and the author of *Talking Back to Prozac: What Doctors Aren't Telling You About Today's Most Controversial Drug,* "The big difference between a dark night of the soul and so-called clinical depression is economics. . . ."If you define depression as an illness, doctors make a living." Furthermore, he adds, "there are no known biological causes of depression. It's all just word games made up by psychiatrists in order to justify medical intervention." Breggin claims that the Food and Drug Administration knows that Prozac is basically a stimulant that can produce an artificial state of euphoria, but the agency has suppressed the information. Additionally, he says, "it's impossible to empower someone spiritually by giving them a pill. The drug keeps them from dealing with life's ultimate issues and from turning to self, others, and God. Love is what ultimately heals us and the world."

Unlike Breggin, Antonio Wood says that depression causes documentable changes in the brain and needs to be addressed biologically. However, he views medication as just one part of the story. "Depression really has three aspects," he explains. In addition to biological changes, depression includes cognitive disturbances, such as poor self-image, and social alienation. "People with depression typically feel separate, isolated, out of community or communion, which is why depression is also a social and spiritual issue," he says, noting that both habitual, negative patterns of thinking and social isolation produce distortions at the molecular level. For this reason, all three aspects must be dealt with in treatment.

"Talking about Prozac is extremely simplistic and misinformed," he says, "because Prozac alone won't do anything." In addition to therapy and medication. Wood's patients participate in a year-long group seminar, which includes cognitive re-education and addresses social and spiritual concerns. What I'm trying to do is create an environment where people will be more engaged," he says. Moreover, because of the multiple ways in which depression alters the body's regulatory systems, Wood's patients are asked to eat three meals a day, exercise regularly, avoid sugar and alcohol completely, and spend an hour each day either in sunlight or under intense artificial light.

Good News and Bad News

With all the fervent discussion about how best to treat depression. I can't help wondering what's really going on. Has our definition of depression expanded? Or are we in fact more depressed than ever?

The answer to both questions is probably yes, speculates Mark Epstein. Not only are clinicians more sensitive to depression and more likely to pick up on it, but the definition of the disorder has also widened beyond a grossly disorganizing and incapacitating illness to include subacute chronic dysthymia, as well as depression associated with childhood and old age. That's the good news: People who in the past would have gone undiagnosed are being successfully treated—with or without antidepressants.

Less reassuring is the news that depression is on the rise. The most important factor in the growing incidence is social isolation, suggests Wood. "We're really social animals. If we're taken out of the pack, we die," he says, citing studies of the Amish in Pennsylvania who became depressed and died after being shunned as outcasts. The same is true of healthy infants who are left alone for long periods of time. According to Wood, the mobility of families, coupled with the breakdown of the nuclear family, is predisposing the entire culture to depression.

Suffering from the Structure

Spiritual teachers with whom I spoke all shared this view. "The social structure of society is the underlying problem," says Dileepji, a Northern California-based teacher of Kundalini Maha yoga. People are so lonely, and there is so little support," he adds. "In India there is a much stronger sense of belonging and community."

What's more, says Rabbi Zalman Schachter of Philadelphia, we're all so busy and stressed out, there's no time to go down into the dungeon and climb back up again. "In every religious society," he notes, "there are built-in periods of grief and mourning, periods when you can have your depression within a liturgical context. The notion that we can function without setting time aside for spiritual self-maintenance is just not right. Whether people are taking Prozac or not, they need to take time to go into themselves and experience the pain and sadness that are part of being human."

MARKETING ANTIDEPRESSANTS

Greg Critser

The popularity of Prozac and other antidepressants may not be attributal primarily to success rates and word-of-mouth publicity from patients, according to Greg Critser. Critser, the former editor of *Buzz* magazine, maintains that drug companies have used unethical means to promote antidepressants without true regard for the safety of the millions of people who have been prescribed these drugs. As a result, he asserts, the companies have received enormous profits while antidepressants have been widely promoted as the best solution to depressive illness. A sufferer of depression himself, Critser expresses his concern over whether he uses antidepressants because they alleviate his symptoms or because drug companies have prompted the desire to ease emotional pain through pills. He presents compelling evidence that pharmaceutical companies may be contributing to the trend toward sanctioning—and even favoring—chemically altered personalities.

Not long ago, while vacationing in the sun-bleached Mexican port town of Manzanillo, I encountered the future of the American medical system. It wasn't a hospital or an HMO. It wasn't even one of those hardscrabble *clinicas* that have become so familiar in parts of Los Angeles or New York or Houston these days. It was a *farmacia* [pharmacy], its owner fanning himself in the midday heat.

"Prozac?" I inquired, using my best gringoese. "Do you carry Prozac?"

"*Si, señor*," replied the druggist. "*Cuanto?*"

How many? Mexican pharmacists have rolled out that beautiful question to curious *norteamericanos* [North Americans] for decades now; what was traditionally preceded by a lengthy doctor's visit and costly prescription in the United States could almost always be secured *mas directamente* [more directly] in Mexico. No questions asked, either. But the difference is fading—when it comes to the availability of drugs, we're starting to look like Mexico. This strange epiphany came to me while I was still in Manzanillo, when I happened across some American magazines and, flipping through them, was struck by the myriad "Ask Your Physician About . . ." advertisements exhorting readers to try new medications for high blood pressure, prostate enlargement, ulcers, and other ailments. "Without a prescription!" advised one. After returning to the United States, I seemed to see proof of the change everywhere. As they say in Hollywood, I'm talking structure here—a health-care system that each day is devoted less to the art of medicine and more to the delivery of pills. Consider:

The Rise of the Pharmaceutical Giants

• In March 1995, Jan Leschly, the chief executive officer of SmithKline Beecham (1995 sales: $11 billion), who is also known in the trade as "the Mike Ovitz of the pharmaceuticals industry," closed his fortieth deal in eighteen months—that's one every two weeks—by acquiring Coastal Healthcare Group, Inc., the largest physician-management group in the country. The result is that SmithKline Beecham, one of the world's largest drug companies, now "covers" 6,000 doctors and 600,000 patients.

• In May 1995, Schein Pharmaceutical and Solvay Pharmaceuticals, makers of several psychopharmacological concoctions, joined forces to form a "mental health group alliance." Their stated goal was "to provide our customers with a more comprehensive line of psycho therapeutic agents at reasonable costs."

• In October 1995, asked about why his company, the pharmaceutical giant Pfizer Inc., *hadn't* yet purchased its own managed-care company, chairman William Steere replied: "[B]ecause we deal with the pharmacy benefit managers. And we have relationship with drugstores. We get wonderful information from drugstores. . . . We can drill down to the patient from any of these centers."

• In November 1995, the General Accounting Office (GAO) released a study of the pharmacy benefit managers (PBMs) Steere referred to. PBMs, which administer the prescription-drug part of health-insurance plans for self-insured employers, insurance companies, and health management organizations (HMOs), provide services to about 50 percent of the population. Because PBMs control the lists of prescription drugs, or formularies, that health plans will pay for, they are attractive to pharmaceutical companies. Indeed, the GAO noted that the five largest PBMs (Medco, Diversified, PCS, Value Rx, and the Prescription Service), which cover 80 million people, were in turn owned by three large pharmaceutical companies (respectively, Merck, Smith Kline Beecham, Eli Lilly) or by companies "in alliance" with one (Pfizer). Under these arrangements, the GAO said, some PBMs had dropped from their formularies medications that competed with drugs manufactured by their parent company or an allied company.

As startling as these developments are, few mainstream news organizations took note; there was no national debate about the possible conflicts of interest that could occur when a company that makes pills might own the companies that oversee the payment and use of them. (In fact, if there was any attention at all paid to the strange new confluences, it was on Wall Street, where the Dow Jones Drug Company Index rose 59 percent in 1995.) No longer content merely to manufacture and sell drugs, pharmaceutical companies (1995 worldwide sales: $700 billion) are drawing ever closer to the end consumer. As a recent issue of *Med Ad News*, the industry's bible, put it, drug companies aren't competing with one another anymore; instead, "they will grow by taking share away from other health care services."

I find this assertion worrisome. Does "taking away" mean from me? From doctors? From hospitals? From the medical institutions Americans used to look to for protection from "market forces"? What, exactly, does Smith Kline Beecham CEO Jan Leschly want from me? Not to put too fine a point on it, but should I be rereading Aldous Huxley's *Brave New World*?

A Personal Interest

To explain how I started asking such about the pharmaceutical industry, I should first describe the nature of my particular ailment, depression, and note that it places me as a consumer in one of the drug industry's fastest-growing markets and thus provides as good a way as any to observe broader forces at work. My ten-year pilgrim's progress through the American health-care system has, on one level, been no progress at all; rather, my treatment has simply changed with the industry itself. . . .

My attempt to deal with depression began with talk therapy, which for most of this century was the norm. American psychiatrists were the great holdouts when it came to medicating the depressed. The Germans, the French, the British never blinked in this regard; treat the symptoms, they said, *then* get to the root. Americans, in their perpetual zeal to "be real," blazed new trails. Manhattan supplanted Vienna, Los Angeles soared into past lives, primal screams, mood therapies. Sturming and dranging, Zenning and koaning, the coasts teemed with searchers. . . .

In eight years of talk therapy, however, I can't escape major depression. I am referred to R., my psychiatrist, by my counselor, who decides that my problem "may be chemical"—in other words, beyond her ken. "Don't worry," she tells me. "He's very conservative with the drugs. He won't give them to you unless you've got to take them." She writes R.'s name and number on a scrap of paper and sends me off.

As it turns out, R. is a short, stout man in his fifties with a quiet demeanor and a slight Brooklyn accent. His office, on the west side of Los Angeles, is in one of those characterless three-story affairs filled with shrinks who got into the profession before HMOs, competing masters of social work, and various self-help gurus took the fun out of it. For three $140 sessions, he and I review family and medical history.

I give him the Cliffs Notes version because the meter is ticking. As I
later find out, this is what R. was writing as I chattered on:

> 6/20/89: "Sporadic severe depression." "Marital stress."
> 7/1/89: "Occasional suicidal ideation." "Rarely cries—yet *looks*
> depressed."
> 7/7/89: "Very depressed. Says he will quit or kill self." "What
> does he do for fun?"
> 7/14/89: "DX depressive neurosis." "Rec. anti-dep.—start
> Norpramin."

And Norpramin works. At least for a while. I say "for a while"
because my condition turns out to be not short-term but chronic. In
this I know I'm far from alone. Many depressed people have much
more tortuous stories than mine. We each have our own firing mechanism—some mysterious yet recognizable, bio-social moment that
triggers the condition. There is hardly a depressed person I know who,
upon learning of the nature of the disease, doesn't say something like,
"It's genetic." Or, "I always knew it ran in the family.". . .

Development of Designer Drugs

How did talk therapy disappear beneath the onslaught of today's
designer drugs? The answer can be found in the busily enterprising
milieu of the mid-Eighties, when three trends converged, creating the
new age of pharmo-capitalism. The first had to do with technology.
For decades medical science had suspected that one cause of depression involved low levels of the brain chemical serotonin. To only
slightly oversimplify, serotonin was thought to act as a connector
between neural transmitters and receivers. The problem, researchers
postulated, was that, in some people, one part of the brain cell known
as the "reuptake pump" was overactive; it automatically hoovered up
too many serotonin particles, leaving the receptors understimulated—
depressed. For researchers, the problem was trying to block that reuptake—thereby leaving more serotonin to do more stimulating—without blocking the uptake of other agents that *should* be sucked up.

But how to test any compounds suspected of having such properties in the first place? The answer was decidedly low-tech. Researchers
at corporate laboratories began injecting rats with various agents
believed to inhibit serotonin uptake. They then ground up the rat
brains and spun them in a centrifuge. The resulting compound, called
a synaptosome, was then exposed to serotonin and other brain chemicals. Scientists stuffed hundreds of such compounds into rats and
then blenderized them. The goal was to find an instance in which the
rat synaptosome sucked up everything but serotonin. In July of 1974,
this is exactly what happened. Researchers at Eli Lilly reported that an
experimental chemical known only as #82816 selectively blocked the
reuptake of neural serotonin. Moreover, the compound appeared to

be pharmaceutically "clean"—it affected few other neural systems, so side effects would be minimal. A note: #82816 was labeled fluoxetine. This is what we now call Prozac. And so it was one of the cheap ironies of our age, with all its tormented concerns about animal rights, that it took a million bloody rats to make us happy again.

Changes in the Industry

What kept Prozac from becoming just another grudgingly used drug in the psychiatrist's dusty apothecary? I recall seeing a photograph in the *New York Times* that goes a long way toward an answer. The date is September 14, 1984. In the photo smile two unlikely congressional allies: the very Representative Henry Waxman of Los Angeles, and the very conservative Senator Orrin Hatch of Utah. The "odd couple," as the *Times*'s imaginative headline writers dubbed them, were captured in full-on Reagan-era oiliness as they donned promotional T-shirts from the Association of Generic Drug Companies. The T-shirts read: "Politics Make Strange Bedfellows." Hatch and Waxman were being feted because they had just shepherded through both houses a piece of legislation that would forever change the character of the pharmaceutical industry. In a thrilling display of political euphemism, they called this the Drug Price Competition and Patent Term Restoration Act of 1984. It was actually a spectacular piece of back-scratching. The act expanded the number of drugs suitable for so-called Abbreviated New Drug Applications, or ANDAs, which were intended to make it easier for cheap generics to reach the market. This is what attracted Waxman. More importantly, the act gave pharmaceutical companies up to five extra years of patent protection—in effect, a new license to print money. This is what attracted Hatch.

But even with new patent protections, pharmaceutical-industry veterans knew the game was changing. In the past, unopposed by an organized generic-drug lobby, they had been free to charge as much as possible. Price, not quantity, ruled the bottom line. Now the most farseeing executives envisioned a new strategy. Capitalizing on the Reagan era's laissez-faire policies, they switched from a strategy of introducing a few new drug applications a year to introducing dozens. They lobbied for, and obtained, permission to use European studies of new drugs to accelerate the process. In 1992 they pushed through the Prescription Drug User Fee Act, which mandated that manufacturers pay fees to process New Drug Applications. The act was billed as the quintessential government-industry partnership. What it *did* was make the Food and Drug Administration (FDA) increasingly dependent on funds designated for the approval of new drugs. By 1995, the agency's review time had shrunk from thirty-three months to nineteen.

Yet even the profits from a wide, fast stream of new drugs would eventually dry up in the face of competition from generics. Marketing executives had to find a way to get more out of their companies' win-

dow of opportunity. In the case of antidepressants, which were traditionally dispensed by the nation's small corps of psychiatrists, the
industry desperately needed to broaden its base of distributors. To do
that, Lilly, Pfizer, and a number of other manufacturers targeted
health-management groups and HMOs, which, as we all now know,
are charged with the dual responsibilities of providing therapy *and*
cutting costs. For them, Prozac was a panacea. Almost immediately,
the average number of insurer-paid visits to talk therapists fell dramatically while drug-therapy numbers soared. By the late Eighties, of
nearly 16 million patients who visited doctors for depression, 70 percent ended up in drug therapy. And slowly but surely, nonpsychiatric
physicians were brought into the prescribing fold. Lilly and other
manufacturers underwrote "mental health days" for area medical
groups. The events were marketed as "educational" forums; they func-
tioned as subsidized marketing for the company and for the physicians. In one program, held in 1993 under the auspices of the American Psychiatric Association and funded by Lilly, 56,000 attendees in
all fifty states were "screened" for depression. Organizers bragged that
"more than 50 percent [of attendees] scored positive for depression
and were referred.". . .

But the ultimate goal of the new pharmo-capitalism involves the
consumer, once known as "the patient." Today, the American patient
is inexorably being transformed into his own pharmacist. The trend is
most apparent in the pages of magazines, with their weirdly text-
heavy ads. Less obvious are the marketing fests taking place in the
nation's doctors' offices and emergency rooms. There one inevitably
hears the cheery, insistent voices of the local "health care" cable station prattling on about how you can have "a better, fuller life" if you
just fill out the self-diagnostic chart about depression that's sitting
right there by your chair. (I once saw a plainly undepressed young
Latino couple filling these out in triplicate, as if they were participating in some kind of medical lotto.)

To get an idea of whom, exactly, the companies view as most
important in this regard, I asked the FDA for a list of all promotional
materials submitted for review by Pfizer Inc., maker of the antidepressant Zoloft. In it were the traditional promotional pieces—an "Anxiety Convention Detail Aid" and a "Depression Pocket Card," presumably something like one of those Miranda warning cards the police on
NYPD Blue are always using—along with a variety of visual aids—a
"somatic depression video" and a "Zoloft Slide Kit" and a "Women's
Synergy" card. Under the heading "Patient Education Materials" were
nineteen separate items, ranging from a "Patient Flip Chart" to a
"Mending the Mind" video. But there were only seven items listed
under "Physician Education Materials."

Not that they feel snubbed. As R. told me one day, "It used to be
whenever I got invited to a seminar, it was box chicken and a speech

in the Neuropsychiatric Institute. Now, it's a *really nice* dinner at Harry's in Century City."

Tragedy and Poetry

Was there a time in human evolution when reuptake pumps were *supposed* to be "overactive"? Did God really want us to have stimulated neurons? I wonder this because one day a few years ago I received a call from my mother. She had been cleaning out some old files and had come across a small, gray monograph entitled "Metaphysical anguish in the poetry of Domenico Stromei." Inside the title page the author had scrawled: "To Elvira, a worthy descendant of a fine poet." Elvira was my grandmother's name; Stromei was her maiden name.

I could hardly read the little book, so dense were its metaphysical allusions, so rich its diagnosis of Stromei's poetry. This, though, I could discern: Stromei was born in 1810 in the impoverished central Italian village of Tocco da Casauria. For the most part, his life had been hard. He was in a constant battle for economic survival, and he was plagued with poor health. He supported himself and his family by working as a cobbler, and it was there, in the cramped confines of his shop, that they say my great-great-great-grand-uncle found his muse. At his little bench, Domenico Stromei developed a new philosophical mode to help him bear life's burdens. This he called *la poesia del dolore* [the poetry of sadness].

Sandro Sticca, the monograph's author, describes *la poesia del dolore:* "In its most visible and concrete form Stromei's philosophy takes its root in the direct observation of reality. . . . In [his] poems the poet comes directly in contact with that reality and he develops a philosophical mode, stoic in essence, which helps him deal with it and bear it. Within this mode is expressed *la poesia del dolore*, a poetry which, transfigured by phantasy and feeling, conquers his pessimism and even the *dolore* itself. . . . [E]ven in the most vehement revolt, the poet returns to a tranquil sense of submission to an inexorable destiny, in a virile and dignified manner." In short, my distant ancestor Domenico accepted tragedy as necessary. Did Domenico's way of looking at the world have an evolutionarily appropriate purpose? Back then, no one could take a pill. And now, doesn't modern capitalism say we have to? Just asking.

Drug Combinations

Most Mondays, when I go to R.'s office, I can count on two things. One, that we will have a pointed, often humorous discussion. This is because R. is a wise, learned man with a Talmudic sense of irony. Two, that we will spend much of our time talking about medication. For most depressed Americans these days, this is typical, as is ongoing experimentation with which drugs might work. For five years R. cycled me through a blizzard of drugs and drug combinations. Among them:

Norpramin; Norpramin with Inderal (to lower high blood pressure caused by the Norpramin); Prozac (at first to counteract the Inderal, which made me depressed); Prozac and Norpramin; Prozac, Norpramin, and Yocon (to alleviate sexual dysfunction caused by the Prozac); Wellbutrin (warning: .01 percent chance of a seizure); Tenormin; Zoloft; Zoloft with Norpramin and Tenormin; Zoloft with Desyrel (warning: possibility of priapism); Desyrel alone; Buspar; Buspar with Desyrel; Buspar with lithium; Paxil with lithium; Paxil, lithium, and acidophilus (for stomachache side effects); Paxil with Pondimin (because Paxil made me eat like a pig); Paxil alone; Paxil with Synthroid (to raise thyroid levels); Serzone; Luvox; Prozac with Synthroid. I continued to get depressed and confronted R., whose chart on me, with its scrawls of "Prozac 10mg^, Norp. 25+, Lith. 10~," looked more like a game plan for the Rose Bowl than a biography of my mind. "Look," I said, "how long does this go on? When do I get rid of this?"

He gave me a patient lecture on how some depressed people are what he called "long-term chronic." "No one knows why really," he went on. "You might be a person for whom depression is ingrained. Very deep." He gave me one of those knowingly raised eyebrows. "It's a day at a time. . . ."

It was not a heartening discussion, and as I drove back to my office, two other words R. used to describe me for the first time come back to haunt me. The words were: "treatment-resistant."

I called Dr. Frank Ayd, who publishes the respected *International Drug Therapy Newsletter*. R. had given me his name as someone who might be able to explain "augmentation drug therapy"—the use of several drugs with a central antidepressant. I expected a long, detailed discourse about how some drugs stimulate neurotransmitters, how some serve to sensitize neuroreceptors, and how the whole process is a search for a scientifically balanced equilibrium.

Instead, Dr. Ayd gave me the biomedical equivalent of a good old chaw over the tobacco spittoon. "My father was a pharmacist," he said, "and he always kept a big jug on the lower counter of his mixing table. Basically, it was a jury-rigged concoction of a bunch of cold and flu remedies that a lot of his patients swore by but that had no official designation. He called it Theriac. And for a lot of his patients with persistent problems it was a wonder. But it was a totally anecdotal concoction."

For a long time, drug combinations for the depressed were looked down on, Ayd told me. But the practice is coming back. "Treatment-resistant depression was not apparent at first. But now we know that the new generation of drugs doesn't work for them on the convenient, one-a-day program the drug companies talk about all the time. And if you talk to the treatment-resistant, you see the suffering. You realize you *have* to experiment. It's heartrending. It's like trying to work with a person with Alzheimers. There are a *lot* of genetic factors here. . . ."

Weaving Webs of Deceit

According to the FDA, the pharmaceutical industry spends more than $10 billion on promotion every year. Our media and medical establishment are drunk on it—from the editorial pages of the *New York Times*, which regularly rents out space to Lilly et al., to the American Medical Association and the American Psychiatric Association, whose members suck up free promo money and research funds. Ten billion dollars, to state the obvious, buys a lot of understanding. This is why, in the marketing departments of *Time* and *Newsweek*, "*up* pill covers are some of our biggest sellers!" as a friend of mine who worked in one of those departments told me recently. A look at the last five years of newsweekly covers reveals few *bummer* pill stories, yet the files of the FDA's Division of Drug Marketing, Advertising, and Communications (DDMAC) are full of horror stories. This division, empowered to review all promotional materials, has a small handicap: because of the First Amendment, it can require submission for review only *after* the company has begun to use the ads. This unregulated window of opportunity has produced a new opportunist—the rogue pharmo-capitalist.

The rogue pharmo-capitalist—also known as a drug company sales representative—differs from his industry antecedents, who went by the folksier monikers of "detail men" or "product reps." Whereas the previous generation relied on a few free samples and an occasional lunch for the buyer, the new generation, emboldened by the media's lack of scrutiny, is, like the witches in *Macbeth*, routinely making up new uses and indications for its potions out of thin air.

Such was the case on September 6, 1994, when the FDA caught representatives of SmithKline Beecham, maker of the antidepressant Paxil, handing out unapproved, homemade promotional materials containing, the FDA said, "numerous false and/or misleading claims." One of the items was a cheery handwritten note, on Paxil stationery, left with physicians. "Dr. [X]. Hello!" it said. "Why should you use Paxil instead of Prozac?" and then went on with such "egregious violations" (the FDA's words) as suggesting that Paxil is safer than Prozac (it is not), that it costs less (only to wholesalers), and that it is easier on the elderly (a claim the FDA found to be, simply, "false"). . . .

Then there is Eli Lilly, maker of Prozac. Lilly's cadre of detail men are the proverbial aluminum-siding salesmen of the antidepressant industry. Their exploits are already legendary. One of the group's more colorful buccaneering adventures was at a "National Depression Awareness Day" held at a suburban Maryland high school. As revealed in 1995 by the *Washington Post*, the day was billed as an educational forum but actually turned into a Prozac referral day, in which Lilly sales representatives distributed promotional pens and brochures, addressed 1,300 students, and presumably went home feeling that their time was well spent.

Hype and Hard Sells

So endemic is the practice of hyping product features the facts clearly don't support that FDA deputy commissioner Mary K. Pendergast, speaking in October 1994 before the House Subcommittee on Regulation, Business Opportunities, and Technology, was moved to uncharacteristically straightforward language. "Promotion of unapproved uses by company sales representatives," she stated, "is a major problem." Yet rogue campaigns get called what they are only when the perpetrators are caught red-handed. The FDA knows that in the new age of do-it-yourself, on-the-run pharmo-capitalism, the game is going to the innovator. And innovate the pharmo-capitalists have done.

Many companies now routinely sponsor trials of approved drugs that, according to a recent paper in the *New England Journal of Medicine*, "serve little or no scientific purpose." There are so-called seeding trials, where thousands of company sales reps fan out to recruit doctors they know prescribe certain drugs, and then pay them for each patient they enroll in a "study" to try a new drug.

So there are salesmen as label writers, studies as sales tools—and pharmacists as arm-twisters. As if doctors weren't getting enough of a hard sell, at least one leading pharmaceutical company, Upjohn, has been caught paying bribes to pharmacists to persuade doctors to switch to new drugs. This the FDA has dubbed a "switch campaign." Another company, Miles, Inc., maker of a hypertension medication, paid pharmacists for identifying patients who were taking older forms of drugs and then sending these patients coupons to help them switch to a new drug.

Who knows where all this innovation will lead? Certainly not the FDA, which is too busy approving new drugs to properly patrol the trenches. Still, a few at the beleaguered agency do get the drift. As commissioner Pendergast told Congress last year, "When I get a prescription filled, I want a drug that will benefit me, not my drugstore and pharmacist."

Is serotonin the mystical spark of the postmodern mind? I ask this because on the night of March 14, 1854, my great-great-great-granduncle Domenico suffered, according to Professor Sticca, "a terrible fall," one made all the worse because Stromei had been ill for the entire previous year. This accident, Sticca writes, precipitated "a definite change of emphasis and an ulterior purpose in his poems." From then on Stromei had a "growing realization of the mysterious nobility and rationality of life within the Christian context." Late in life he became fond of taking long walks to the town cemetery and frequenting a Renaissance-era church in Tocco called La Chiesa della Madonna delle Grazie. The church was founded by monks of the Dominican order and so was imbued with the essence of the order's brand of spirituality: to study, to contemplate, to preach, to adore the Virgin. In the center of the church stands a remarkable statue of the Virgin and Child, She in blissful contemplation, He in cherubically animated oratory.

I find myself, in the midst of my depression, imagining my distant ancestor as he gazes upon this statue. He is an old man who has lost his beloved wife. He is poor and ill. Yet his muse is more vibrant than ever. For him, anguish, stoically confronted, has become the search for a deeper way of life. I imagine Domenico thinking, perhaps, of the words of Thomas Aquinas, the first great interpreter of St. Domenic, his namesake. *"Contemplare, et contemplata aliis tradere,"* Aquinas wrote. "Gaze with love on God; share what has been seen with others."

But that way of handling melancholy, for better or for worse, is not what premillennial America is all about. It's not what *I* am about; I am someone who takes a pill for my sorrows. I wonder, though, if my depression is "unbearable" without medication only because I know that this medication exists. I also wonder if the drugs are preventing me from finding the solace Domenico did. Who am I now without medication? Will I ever know?

Perhaps not—by Spring 1996 my suffering was somewhat dulled. My mood swings had ebbed. So had the incredible self-hatred that inevitably followed any success. I was on a straight regimen of Prozac, 40 mg. Nothing fancy. There are side effects; they show. I have put on weight, and there is a lethargy to my manner that surprises some of my acquaintances. At this point I'm inclined to believe that, depression-wise, this may be my state of the art. Still, R. indirectly holds out promise when he tells me, "To be honest, I've *never* seen you anything less than mildly depressed."

And if some terrific new pill comes along, I will read about it every-where, and if I want it—*cuanto?*—I will be able to have it, and in doing so I will be a very regular late-twentieth-century American in good graces with my health-care provider. Cocaine and Sigmund Freud ushered in the twentieth century, but now the culture has no time for the second part of that equation. There is no time for talk. No insurance money for it either. Serotonin enhancement and PBMs will ring in the twenty-first century.

Meanwhile, the pharmo-capitalists busily plan their next beach-head. The global market for antidepressants is expected to reach more than $6 billion by 1998—having doubled in four years. Two new anti-depressants are pending FDA approval, four are in the late stages of development, and six are right behind them in the pipeline. And so it is that *Med Ad News*'s "Executive Edition," an insider's report to phar-maceutical-company leaders, recently described the "winning traits" of the next century's most profitable drug companies: "The winning pharmaceutical companies will have to gain direct access to these cus-tomers . . . the pharmaceutical company of the future will have to interface with the patient."

The future, it appears, draws ever nearer.

ORGANIZATIONS TO CONTACT

The editors have compiled the following list of organizations concerned with the issues debated in this book. The descriptions are derived from materials provided by the organizations. All have publications or information available for interested readers. The list was compiled on the date of publication of the present volume; the information provided here may change. Be aware that many organizations take several weeks or longer to respond to inquiries, so allow as much time as possible.

American Association of Suicidology
4201 Connecticut Ave. NW, Suite 310, Washington, DC 20008
(202) 237-2280 • fax: (202) 237-2282
e-mail: amyjomc@ix.netcom.com
web address: http://www.cyberpsych.org/aas/index.html

The association is one of the largest suicide prevention organizations in the nation. It believes that suicidal thoughts are usually a symptom of depression and that suicide is rarely a rational decision. The association provides referrals to regional crisis centers in the United States and Canada and helps those grieving the death of a loved one to suicide. It publishes numerous pamphlets and reports.

American Psychiatric Association (APA)
1400 K St. NW, Washington, DC 20005
(202) 682-6000 • fax: (202) 682-6850
e-mail: apa@psych.org • web address: http://www.psych.org

An organization of psychiatrists dedicated to studying the nature, treatment, and prevention of mental disorders, the APA helps create mental health policies, distributes information about psychiatry, and promotes psychiatric research and education. It publishes the *American Journal of Psychiatry* and *Psychiatric Services* monthly.

American Psychological Association
750 First St. NE, Washington, DC 20002-4242
(202) 336-5500 • fax: (202) 336-5708
e-mail: public.affairs@apa.org • web address: http://www.apa.org

This society of psychologists aims to "advance psychology as a science, as a profession, and as a means of promoting human welfare." It produces numerous publications, including the monthly journal *American Psychologist*, the monthly newspaper *APA Monitor*, and the quarterly *Journal of Abnormal Psychology*.

Citizens Commission on Human Rights (CCHR)
6362 Hollywood Blvd., Los Angeles, CA 90028
(800) 869-2247 • (213) 467-4242 • fax: (213) 467-3720
e-mail: humanrights@cchr.org • web address: http://www.cchr.org

CCHR is a nonprofit organization that works to expose and eradicate criminal acts and human rights abuses by psychiatry. The organization believes that psychiatric drugs actually cause insanity and violence. Its members believe their duty is to "expose and help abolish any and all physically damaging practices in the field of mental healing." CCHR publishes nine books, including *Psychiatry: Destroying Morals* and *Psychiatry: Education's Ruin*.

International Society for the Study of Dissociation
60 Ravere Dr., Suite 500, Northbrook, IL 60062
(847) 480-0899 • fax: (847) 480-9282
e-mail: info@issd.org • web address: http://www.issd.org

The society's membership comprises mental health professionals and students interested in dissociation. It conducts research and promotes improved understanding of these conditions. It publishes the quarterly journal *Dissociation* and a quarterly newsletter.

National Association of Psychiatric Health Systems
web address: http://www.naphs.org

The association represents the interests of private psychiatric hospitals, residential treatment centers, and programs partially consisting of hospital care. It provides a forum for ideas concerning the administration, care, and treatment of the mentally ill and it publishes various fact sheets and policy recommendations, including *How You Can Help Reform Mental Health: A Grassroots Guide to Political Action*.

National Depressive and Manic Depressive Association
730 N. Franklin St., Suite 501, Chicago, IL 60610-3526
(312) 642-0049 • fax: (312) 642-7243
e-mail: MYRTIS@aol.com

The association provides support and advocacy for patients with depression and manic-depressive illness. It seeks to persuade the public that these disorders are biochemical in nature and to end the stigmatization of people who suffer from them. It publishes the quarterly *NDMDA Newsletter* and various books and pamphlets.

National Foundation for Depressive Illness (NAFDI)
PO Box 2257, New York, NY 10116
recorded message: (800) 248-4344
web address: http://www.depression.org

NAFDI seeks to inform the public, health care providers, and corporations about depression and manic-depressive illness. It promotes the view that these disorders are physical illnesses treatable with medication, and it believes that such medication should be made readily available to those who need it. The foundation maintains several toll-free telephone lines and distributes brochures, bibliographies, and literature on the symptoms of and treatments for depression and manic-depressive illness. It also publishes the quarterly newsletter *NAFDI News*.

National Institute of Mental Health (NIMH)
NIMH Public Inquiries
5600 Fishers Ln., Room 7C-02, MSC 8030, Bethesda, MD 20892-8030
e-mail: nimhinfo@nih.gov • web address: http://www.nimh.nih.gov

NIMH is the federal agency concerned with mental health research. It plans and conducts a comprehensive program of research relating to the causes, prevention, diagnosis, and treatment of mental illnesses. The institute also produces various informational publications on mental disorders and their treatment.

National Mental Health Association
1021 Prince St., Alexandria, VA 22314-2971
(703) 684-7722 • fax: (703) 684-5968
e-mail: nmhainfo@aol.com • web address: http://www.nmha.org

The association is a consumer advocacy organization concerned with combating mental illness and improving mental health. It promotes research into the treatment and prevention of mental illness, monitors the quality of care provided to the mentally ill, and provides educational materials on mental illness and mental health. It publishes the monthly newsletter *The Bell* as well as various pamphlets and reports.

National Resource Center on Homelessness and Mental Illness
Policy Research Associates, Inc.
262 Delaware Ave., Delmar, NY 12054
(800) 444-7415 • fax: (518) 439-7612
e-mail: nrc@prainc.com • web address: http://www.prainc.com/nrc

The center provides information and technical assistance to various agencies concerned with the housing and other needs of the homeless mentally ill. It publishes *Access*, a quarterly newsletter that provides information on research, programs, and initiatives affecting the homeless mentally ill. It also provides free information packets on request.

Obsessive Compulsive Foundation
PO Box 70, Milford, CT 06460-0070
(203) 878-5669 • fax: (203) 874-2826
e-mail: info@ocfoundation.org
web address: http://www.ocfoundation.org

The foundation consists of individuals with obsessive-compulsive disorders (OCDs), their friends and families, and the professionals who treat them. It seeks to increase public awareness of and discover a cure for obsessive-compulsive disorders. It publishes the bimonthly *OCD Newsletter* and brochures and educational materials on OCDs.

Suicide Awareness/Voices of Education (SA/VE)
PO Box 24507, Minneapolis, MN 55424-0507
(612) 946-7998
e-mail: save@winternet.com • web address: http://www.save.org

"The mission of SA/VE is to educate about the brain diseases that, if untreated medically and psychologically, can result in suicide death. To make statements by members' presence through events like the Annual Awareness Day, protest, letter writing, or other activities. To honor the memory of people who died by suicide. To eliminate the stigma on suicide."

World Federation for Mental Health
1021 Prince St., Alexandria, VA 22314
fax: (703) 519-7648
e-mail: wfmh@erols.com • web address: http://www.wfmh.com

The federation is dedicated to improving public mental health worldwide and it strives to coordinate mental health organizations and enhance mental health care in developing countries. It publishes a newsletter four times a year.

BIBLIOGRAPHY

Books

Richard Abrams	*Electroconvulsive Therapy.* New York: Oxford, 1997.
Stephen Arterburn	*Hand-Me-Down Genes and Second-Hand Emotions.* New York: Simon & Schuster, 1994.
E. Edward Beckham and William R. Leber	*Handbook of Depression.* New York: Guilford Press, 1995.
Harold H. Bloomfield	*Hypericum and Depression.* Los Angeles: Prelude, 1996.
Peter Breggin	*Talking Back to Prozac: What Doctors Won't Tell You About Today's Most Controversial Drug.* New York: St. Martin's, 1994.
David D. Burns	*Feeling Good: The New Mood Therapy.* New York: Avon Books, 1992.
David B. Cohen	*Out of the Blue: Depression and Human Nature.* New York: W.W. Norton, 1994.
Kenneth Craig and Keith S. Dobson, eds.	*Anxiety and Depression in Adults and Children.* Thousand Oaks, CA: Sage, 1995.
Kathy Cronkite	*On the Edge of Darkness: Conversations About Conquering Depression.* New York: Doubleday, 1994.
Leon Crytryn	*Growing Up Sad: Childhood Depression and Its Treatment.* New York: W.W. Norton, 1996.
Kedar Nath Dwivedi and Ved Varma	*Depression in Children and Adolescents.* San Diego: Singular Publications, 1997.
Debra Elfenbein ed.	*Living with Prozac and Other Selective Serotonin Reuptake Inhibitors (SSRIs): Personal Accounts of Life on Anti-depressants.* San Francisco: HarperSanFrancisco, 1995.
William Edward Hulme	*Wrestling with Depression: A Spiritual Guide to Reclaiming Life.* Minneapolis: Augsburg, 1995.
Dana Crowley Jack	*Silencing the Self: Women and Depression.* New York: HarperPerennial, 1993.
David Allen Karp	*Speaking of Sadness: Depression, Disconnection, and the Meanings of Illness.* New York: Oxford University Press, 1996.
Donald F. Klein	*Understanding Depression.* New York: Oxford University Press, 1993.
Peter D. Kramer	*Listening to Prozac.* New York: Viking, 1993.
John J. Miletich	*Depression: A Multimedia Sourcebook.* Westport, CT: Greenwood Press, 1995.
Francis Mondimore	*Depression: The Mood Disease.* Baltimore: Johns Hopkins University Press, 1993.
Michael T. Murray	*Natural Alternatives to Prozac.* New York: Morrow, 1996.

Michael J. Norden   *Beyond Prozac: Brain-Toxic Lifestyles, Natural Antidotes and New Generation Antidepressants.* New York: Regan Books, 1995.

Richard O'Connor   *Undoing Depression: What Therapy Doesn't Teach You and Medication Can't Give You.* Boston: Little, Brown, 1997.

Theresa D. O'Nell   *Disciplined Hearts: History, Identity, and Depression in an American Indian Community.* Berkeley and Los Angeles: University of California Press, 1996.

Patricia Owen   *I Can See Tomorrow: A Guide for Living with Depression.* Center City, MN: Hazelden, 1995.

Demitri F. Papolos   *Overcoming Depression.* New York: HarperPerennial, and Janice Papolos   1997.

Terrence Real   *I Don't Want to Talk About It: Overcoming the Secret Legacy of Male Depression.* New York: Scribner, 1997.

David H. Rosen   *Transforming Depression: A Jungian Approach Using Creative Expression.* New York: Putnam, 1994.

Laura Epstein Rosen   *When Someone You Love is Depressed: How to Help Your Loved One Without Losing Yourself.* New York: Free Press, 1996.

Martin E.P. Seligman   *The Optimistic Child.* Boston: Houghton Mifflin, 1995.

Wilfrid Sheed   *In Love with Daylight: A Memoir of Recovery.* New York: Simon & Schuster, 1995.

Andrew E. Slaby   *No One Saw My Pain: Why Teens Kill Themselves.* New York: W.W. Norton, 1994.

William Styron   *Darkness Visible: A Memoir of Madness.* New York: Random House, 1990.

Verta A. Taylor   *Rock-a-by Baby: Feminism, Self Help, and Postpartum Depression.* New York: Routledge, 1996.

Peter C. Whybrow   *A Mood Apart.* New York: HarperCollins, 1997.

Periodicals

Jerry Adler   "A Dose of Virtual Prozac," *Newsweek*, February 7, 1994.

Patricia Lopez Baden   "Beyond the Blues," *Better Homes and Gardens*, September 1995.

Harold H. Bloomfield   "Treating Depression with Hypericum," *Saturday Evening Post*, November/December 1997.

Jane Brody   "Depressed Parents' Children at Risk," *New York Times*, March 3, 1998.

Barry Brophy   "Kindergartners in the Prozac Nation," *U.S. News & World Report*, November 13, 1995.

Michael Castleman   "Becoming Unblued," *Mother Jones*, May/June 1997.

Mary H. Cooper   "Prozac Controversy," *CQ Researcher*, August 19, 1994. Available from 1414 22nd St. NW, Washington, DC 20037.

Geoffrey Cowler   "The Culture of Prozac," *Newsweek*, February 7, 1994.

Mary Crowley   "Do Kids Need Prozac?" *Newsweek*, October 20, 1997.

Susan E. Dubuque   "Fighting Childhood Depression," *Education Digest*,
                         February 1998.

Julia Duin   "Depression . . . or Indulgence?" *Insight*, June 23,
                         1997. Available from P.O. Box 581367, Minneapolis,
                         MN 55458-1367

Susan Enfield   "Jack Dreyfus's Long and Not Unhappy Second Life,"
                         New York, August 26, 1996.

Jan Flatwater   "The Faces of Depression," *Teen*, September 1997.

Kim C. Flodin   "Why New Moms Get the Blues," *Parents*, May 1994.

Greg Gutfeld   "When Depression Strikes . . . Him," *Prevention*,
                         September 1996.

Swanee Hunt and   "I Couldn't Reach My Daughter," *Good Housekeeping*,
Lillian Hunt-Meeks   November 1996.

Stanley Jacobson   "Overselling Depression to the Old Folks," *Atlantic
                         Monthly*, April 1995.

Kay Redfield Jamison   "Manic-Depression: Illness and Creativity," *Scientific
                         American*, February 1995.

Walter Kirn   "Living the Pharmaceutical Life," *Time*, September 29,
                         1997.

Jay Kist   "Dealing with Depression," *Current Health 2*, January
                         1997.

Bernard Kliska and   "Coping with a Leader's Depression," *Nation's
John L. Ward   Business*, July 1996.

Mark S. Lachs   "Depression Isn't Always in Your Head," *Prevention*,
                         May 1998.

Warren Leary   "Depression Travels in Disguise with Other Illnesses,"
                         New York Times, January 17, 1996.

Karen Levine   "Childhood Depression," *Parents*, October 1995.

Doug Marlette   "Hey, Man—Lighten Up!" *Esquire*, September 1996.

Alfred Meyer   "Listening to Paxil," *Psychology Today*, July/August
                         1996.

Carol Potera   "Prozac of the Sea," *Psychology Today*, May/June 1996.

M.E. Rice   "Depression Strengthened Our Family," *Glamour*,
                         September 1997.

Sarah Scott   "Biology and Mental Health: Why Do Women Suffer
                         More Depression and Anxiety?" *Maclean's*, January
                         12, 1998.

Joel P. Smith   "Depression: Darker Than Darkness," *American
                         Scholar*, September 1997.

Elizabeth Somer   "Eating to Beat the Blues," *Better Homes and Gardens*,
                         May 1996.

Elizabeth Stone   "The Anguish of the Depressive Personality,"
                           Cosmopolitan, July 1996.

Ron Taffel   "When Dad Gets the Blues," *Parents,* June 1997.

Joan Vennochi   "When Depression Comes to Work," *Working Woman*,
                           August 1995.

Leslie Vreeland   "New Way to Defeat Depression," *Good Housekeeping*,
                           September 1996.

Diane Marie Weathers   "Death of a Superwoman," *Essence*, March 1998.

Michael D. Yapko   "The Art of Avoiding Depression," *Psychology Today*,
                           May/June 1997.

INDEX